D1408341

Madagascar

*An Agenda for Growth
and Poverty Reduction*

*The World Bank
Washington, D.C.*

World Bank Country Studies are among the many reports originally prepared for internal use as part of the continuing analysis by the Bank of the economic and related conditions of its developing member countries and of its dialogues with the governments. Some of the reports are published in this series with the least possible delay for the use of governments and the academic, business and financial, and development communities. The typescript of this paper therefore has not been prepared in accordance with the procedures appropriate to formal printed texts, and the World Bank accepts no responsibility for errors. Some sources cited in this paper may be informal documents that are not readily available.

The findings, interpretations, and conclusions expressed in this paper are entirely those of the author(s) and should not be attributed in any manner to the World Bank, to its affiliated organizations, or to members of its Board of Executive Directors or the countries they represent. The World Bank does not guarantee the accuracy of the data included in this publication and accepts no responsibility for any consequence of their use. The boundaries, colors, denominations, and other information shown on any map in this volume do not imply on the part of the World Bank Group any judgment on the legal status of any territory or the endorsement or acceptance of such boundaries.

The material in this publication is copyrighted. The World Bank encourages dissemination of its work and will normally grant permission promptly.

Permission to photocopy items for internal or personal use, for the internal or personal use of specific clients, or for educational classroom use, is granted by the World Bank provided that the appropriate fee is paid directly to Copyright Clearance Center, Inc., 222 Rosewood Drive, Danvers, MA 01923, U.S.A., telephone 978 750 8400, fax 978 750 4470. Please contact Copyright Clearance Center prior to photocopying items.

For permission to reprint individual articles or chapters, please fax your request with complete information to the Republication Department, Copyright Clearance Center, fax 978 750 4470.

All other queries on rights and licenses should be addressed to the World Bank at the address above, or fax no. 202 522 2422.

ISBN: 0-8213-4551-6
ISSN: 0253-2123

Library of Congress Cataloging-in-Publication Data

Madagascar, an agenda for growth and poverty reduction
      p.   cm. — (A World Bank country study)
  Includes bibliographical references.
  ISBN 0-8213-4551-6
  1. Poverty—Madagascar.   2. Privatization—Madagascar.
 3. Madagascar—Economic policy.   I. Series.
HC895.Z9P62   1999
  338.9691—dc21   99-32772
                                        CIP

TABLES

BOXES

GRAPHS

STATISTICAL ANNEX

This report is based on the findings of various economic missions that visited Madagascar. The main mission took place in March 1997.

The report was conceived and managed by Ali Mansoor through the first draft (December 1997). Subsequent management was handled by Juan Zalduendo. Contributions were provided by Emmanuel Cuvillier, Paulo de Sa, Marianne Fay, Vicente Ferrer, Raju Kalidindi, Christos Kostopoulos, Herminia Martinez, Branko Milanovic, Alasane N'diaye, Nelly Rabotoson, Dieudonné Randriamanampisoa, Luc Razafimandimby, Mao Sin, and Yves Wong.

Hafez Ghanem and David Yuravlivker were the Peer Reviewers.

The Country Director was Michael Sarris, the Resident Representative was Philippe Le Houerou, and the Sector Manager was Luca Barbone.

The report was processed by Cécile Wodon, Jagdish Lal, and Gboku Lumbila.

ABSTRACT

Madagascar's GDP has grown for 3 decades at an annual average rate of 0.5 percent. Low GDP growth and population increases of about 3 percent annually have led to a continuous decline in living standards — consumption per capita in 1997 US dollars has slipped from US$473 in 1970 to US$227 in 1997. As a result, poverty has worsened, from affecting 40 percent of the population to affecting about 75 percent. This decline in per capita GDP and the corresponding increase in poverty are shocking given the natural endowments of the country, and can be traced to the impact of policies of economic nationalism and extensive State intervention.

Since the second half of the 1980s, government authorities have adopted more pragmatic economic policies. But the pursuit of reforms has at times been too hesitant and even evidenced periods of backtracking. The report highlights that eliminating this dubitative approach towards reform is essential. More specifically, to succeed Madagascar must foster a supply response for private sector development (discussed in Chapter 2); and redefine the role of the public sector (addressed in Chapter 3). The *former* entails focussing on measures that will gain the confidence of both domestic and foreign investors, as the private sector still distrusts the country's paternalistic State which dispenses favors and has a discretionary, selective, and controlling attitude toward private sector development. This requires opening up the economy to foreign investment and know-how, restoring the credibility of the judiciary, creating an investor-friendly administrative and regulatory environment with minimum State involvement, and reducing direct government interests in productive economic activities. The *latter* requires to redefine the role of the State, with concrete actions both on revenues and expenditures, as well as on institutional and organizational areas. Tax revenues need to be increased from 9 percent of GDP in 1997 to around 15 percent by late next decade to finance many unmet developmental needs. Much of this revenue increase should be accomplished through expanding the tax base and improving tax administration. Action is also required on the expenditure side to supply more and better health services; to raise the human capital of the population, mainly in primary education and vocational training; and to improve basic infrastructure, particularly the road network. This should be accomplished first and foremost by increases in efficiency.

In sum, the Malagasy State needs to transform itself to encourage individual initiative, to provide the poor with the means to participate in economic life, and to support the development of the private sector, domestic or foreign. Madagascar must both look to its own history to learn about what does not work, and look to the example of other countries that have succeeded in lifting themselves from poverty to identify what does work. Ultimately, to revert its poor performance Madagascar needs to assume ownership of a profound and convincing reform program.

	1991	1992	1993	1994	1995	1996	1997
FMG/US$ (average)	1,835	1,864	1,914	3,083	4,268	4,055	5,093

WEIGHTS AND MEASURES

Metric system

ACRONYMS AND ABBREVIATIONS

ADEMA	Aéroports de Madagascar	IBRD	International Bank for Reconstruction and Development
AGETIPA	Agence d'Exécution des Travaux d'Intérêt Public d'Antananarivo		
		IDA	International Development Association
AUXIMAD	Société Auxiliaire Maritime de Madagascar	IMF	International Monetary Fund
BFV	Commercial Bank (Banky Fampandrosoana ny Varotra)	INSTAT	National Institute of Statistics
BTM	National Rural Development Bank (Bankin'ny tantsana Mpamokatra)	JPY	Japanese yen
		LDCs	Less-developed countries
		LF	Loi de finance
CAB	Current account balance	NCT	Net current transfers
CBM	Central Bank of Madagascar	NGO	Nongovernmental organization
CFPE	Centre Fiscal Pilote des Entreprises		
		OMNIS	Office Militaire National des Industries Stratégiques
CMN	Compagnie Maritime de Navigation	PEs	Public enterprises
CPI	Consumer price index	PIP	Public investment program
DEM	Deutsche mark	PM	Prime Minister
ENMG	Ecole Nationale de la Magistrature et des Greffes	QIT/RTZ	Quebec Iron Titane / Río Tinto Company
EU	European Union	SAF	Structural adjustment facility
EPZ	Export Processing Zone	SDR	Special drawing rights
ESAF	Enhanced Structural Adjustment Facility	SMTM	Société Malgache des Transports Maritimes
FDI	Foreign direct investment	SOFITRANS	Société Financière pour le Développement du Transport et du Tourisme
FF	French franc		
FMG	Malagasy franc		
GBP	British pound	UNDP	United Nations Development Program
GDP	Gross domestic product		
GFS	Goods and factor services	US	United States
GNFS	Goods and non-factor services	USD/ US$	United States dollar
		VAT	Value-added tax

FISCAL YEAR

January 1–December 31

Vice President:	Callisto Madavo
Country Director:	Michael Sarris
Sector Manager:	Luca Barbone
Country Economist:	Juan Zalduendo

EXECUTIVE SUMMARY

Economic Performance has been Dismal Despite Madagascar's Potential

During the last three decades, Madagascar's GDP has grown at an annual average rate of 0.5 percent, exceeding those only of Niger, Nicaragua, Haiti, and Kiribati. Low GDP growth and population increases of about 3 percent annually have led to a continuous decline in living standards — consumption per capita in 1997 US dollars has slipped by more than half, from US$473 in 1970 to US$227 in 1997. As a result, poverty has worsened, from affecting 40 percent of the population to affecting about 75 percent. Investment in Madagascar during this period has averaged only about 10 percent of GDP; the quality of human capital has deteriorated, evidenced in part by a fall from almost universal primary school enrollment to enrollments of about 73 percent; and the country's physical infrastructure has decayed — for example, the road network of more than 15,000 miles at independence in 1960 now measures about 10,000 miles, much of it in very poor condition.

The decline in per capita GDP and the corresponding increase in poverty are shocking given the natural endowments of the country. Madagascar has rich mineral deposits, fertile land with plentiful rain, and a coastal perimeter of about 3,000 miles that provides access to rich maritime resources. Its unique ecosystem, varied topography, and different climatic zones should also make it attractive to a broad range of tourists. But key economic sectors such as mining and tourism have remained dormant for decades, mainly because of the shortcomings of the business environment, which have been ineffectively and often reluctantly addressed by government. Madagascar's poor economic performance reflects the impact of policies of economic nationalism and self-sufficiency that isolated the country during the 1970s and most of the 1980s, and also of extensive State intervention in economic activities. These policies included price controls to complement public enterprise monopolies; an overvalued exchange rate defended by restrictions on external trade and unsustainable foreign borrowing; budget deficits financed by money creation; and a tax system heavily dependent on the taxation of exports and imports.

Hesitant Reforms are Insufficient for Rapid Recovery

Since the second half of the 1980s, but with some exceptions after 1991, government authorities have adopted more pragmatic economic policies. The exchange rate now floats freely, and the country has set up a *zone franche* to attract export-oriented investment. Foreign investment has risen from virtually zero at the start of the period to US$14 million in 1997, or about one-third of 1 percent of GDP. Private investment has increased to about 5 percent of GDP, though it is still lower than public investment, which was about 7 percent of GDP in

1997. The tax structure is more efficient than in the early 1990s, notably showing an increased reliance on revenues from value-added tax and the elimination of external trade taxes. Non-traditional exports such as those by the fisheries sector and the export-processing zone have also performed well, and have increased their share of total exports from about 25 percent to more than 85 percent.

At times, however, policies have been less decisive. For example, the implementation of Madagascar's privatization program has proceeded very slowly: by mid-1998, no privatizations had occurred and the first significant ones are now likely to take place only in 1999. Direct government intervention in many economic activities has been maintained or even restored. The country also experienced periods of high inflation during the 1990s, damaging confidence in the economy. As a result, growth has alternated between the promising rates of the late 1980s — although even these were barely sufficient to match population growth — and new episodes of stagnation during the first half of the 1990s. Economic growth improved in 1996 and 1997, but is still insufficient given the country's high rates of population growth. The slow implementation of reforms, and the consequent lack of a convincing signal that Madagascar has left behind its failed policies of the past, has contributed to this erratic economic performance.

A Strategy to Break the Vicious Cycle of Poverty

The challenge is clear. Unless the country can close the gap between performance and potential, poverty will continue to affect a large share of the Malagasy population for many generations. Poverty is tied to wealth and income distribution, and to high population growth rates. It manifests itself crudely through the many health, education, and housing deficiencies that affect much of the Malagasy population. Escaping from the poverty trap requires that the country put in place the conditions that would enable it to attain high economic growth rates.

Madagascar can and should aspire to growth rates much higher than the recent average of Sub-Saharan Africa of about 4.5 percent a year. If the country can overcome its reluctance to confront those economic sectors and individuals that have benefited from being protected against competition, and if it can abandon its negative attitude toward foreign direct investment, then growth rates of about 7.5 percent are possible by the middle of the next decade. A 7.5 percent growth rate would enable Madagascar to reduce the number of people suffering from poverty from about 75 percent of the population to less than half by the year 2015. However, this high growth path also entails important hurdles. To succeed, Madagascar must:

- foster a supply response for private sector development (discussed in Chapter 2); and

- redefine the role of the public sector (addressed in Chapter 3).

To *foster a supply response*, Madagascar needs to focus on measures that will gain the confidence of both domestic and foreign investors. Investors distrust the country's paternalistic State which dispenses favors and which has a discretionary, selective, and controlling attitude toward private sector development. As recently as April 1998, the government was still allocating ad hoc tariff and tax exemptions, affecting the business environment in key economic sectors such as rice and sugar and sending mixed signals about its commitment to private sector development.

For the government to become a reliable partner, the government must eliminate corruption, restore the credibility of the judiciary, and create an investor-friendly administrative and regulatory environment that requires minimum involvement of the State. Action in these areas needs to be pragmatic, however. While strengthening the judicial system is imperative, it will take many years to correct the harm wrought by decades of weakness. In addition to policies designed to provide results in the long-term, Madagascar may therefore benefit from mechanisms that aim at rapidly increasing the confidence of the private sector — even if these are temporary solutions. For example, an arbitration system for resolving commercial disputes is worth considering as an interim measure to increase investor confidence.

Direct government involvement in economic activities should be curtailed, and support to private sector development should exclude any mechanisms that distort resource allocation. The country should also pursue a transparent process of privatization, which would eliminate the waste caused by inefficient public enterprises but more importantly would provide an example of efficiency that would stimulate the private sector. This has been the experience of high-growth countries, and is especially relevant in today's global economy, where inefficient resource allocation is forcefully penalized. The privatization process should also create a competitive environment — particularly in the service sector, which has an indirect impact on most other sectors of the economy. Madagascar has announced an ambitious reform program that includes privatization of many economic sectors, but while this agenda is a step in the right direction, it has yet to materialize.

The *role of the public sector* should be redefined and the sector modernized. Action is required on revenues and expenditures, and in institutional and organizational areas. Tax revenues need to be increased from 9 percent of GDP in 1997 to around 15 percent by late next decade, and total government revenues from 9.5 percent to 17 percent of GDP. This is necessary to finance many unmet developmental needs, and to reduce to more sustainable levels fiscal deficits before grants. To avoid crowding out the private sector, however, much of this revenue increase should be accomplished through expanding the tax base and improving tax administration. The tax structure in Madagascar is relatively modern after many years of reforms introduced at the recommendation of Bretton Woods institutions, but ad hoc exemptions, weak enforcement, and tax fraud curtail its potential benefits.

Non-tax revenues are also a potentially important source of revenue, and should be increased from 0.5 percent of GDP to about 2 percent by late next decade. These revenues include license fees for mining and fishing. Allocation of these licenses is not transparent, however, and most revenues are channeled not through Treasury accounts but direct to the corresponding sector ministries.

Action is required on the expenditure side to supply more and better health services; to raise the human capital of the population through increased expenditures, mainly in primary education and vocational training; and to improve basic infrastructure, particularly the road network. Madagascar has a relatively small public sector, with total expenditures, including interest payments, close to 17 percent of GDP. The country currently spends about US$4 per capita on public health matters and US$8 on public education expenditures — about half the amounts considered appropriate for low-income countries. It is necessary to increase these amounts, and the government introduced changes in 1997 and 1998 aimed at doing so, but increasing them effectively requires a strategy that addresses not only the low levels of expenditure but also the effectiveness of these expenditures. If weaknesses in these government social-sector programs are not first eliminated, then the likelihood is high that the impact of any increased expenditure in these programs would be significantly dampened.

If increased revenue collection is not to be wasted, then the public sector must first significantly increase its efficiency. This requires many institutional and organizational changes. Establishing a more transparent administration of public finances and more budgetary discipline rank high among the tasks that lie ahead, and are necessary not only to support a higher level of expenditure but also as a signal of change and political modernization. A more sensible organization of the civil service must be made such that the number of public servants directly serving the Malagasy population is increased. Deconcentration of the central administration, and decentralization in the provision of public goods and services are also crucial for Madagascar's economic and social development since they will serve to better match needs and resources.

In addition to decisive action in the two policy areas mentioned above, Madagascar must recover lost ground by *reversing its negative attitude toward foreign direct investment* (FDI). While much has been done in recent years to encourage foreign investment, particularly in the tourism and mining sectors, the policies introduced are too timid to have brought about significant changes in FDI levels. Madagascar's most important incentive for increasing FDI is to increase its economic efficiency, but higher levels of FDI also bring other benefits. The introduction of new technologies and know-how is a necessary condition for high growth in countries that need to modernize their capital base, and has the added advantage of enabling access to foreign markets. It is only by increasing FDI that Madagascar will increase — in the short- and medium-term — both consumption and investment, and thus make this change.

The country must also show a positive attitude toward visitors from abroad, the benefits of which extend beyond the development of the tourism sector. In this regard, the visa changes introduced in 1997 are a welcome event that, together with partial air transport liberalization, have resulted in an increase in the number of tourists arriving in Madagascar of about 35 percent relative to 1996. Similarly, foreign exchange earnings from the tourism sector peaked in 1997 at about US$60 million, 28 percent more than the previous year. Additional increases are likely before tourist accommodations reach saturation point.

Are there any alternatives to an ambitious and committed transformation of Madagascar's economy? If Madagascar continues with the slow reform program of the last few years, growth rates averaging recent Sub-Saharan African standards could still be achieved and, with luck, sustained. But it is unlikely that consumption per capita could increase significantly under these conditions: high poverty would continue to prevail. It is therefore of the utmost importance that the government acts decisively to evince the break with past attitudes and policies that would positively affect private sector confidence.

Concluding Remarks

The Malagasy State needs to transform itself to encourage individual initiative, to provide the poor with the means to participate in economic life, and to support the development of the private sector, domestic or foreign-invested. Madagascar must both look to its own history to learn about what does not work, and look to the example of other countries that have succeeded in lifting themselves from poverty to identify what does work. To reverse its dismal performance, the country ultimately requires a government and civil society that assume ownership of a profound and convincing program of economic transformation.

What is the role of the international community? Donor assistance should be generous, given Madagascar's many needs, but experience suggests that donor resources are only effective in those countries where the will for reform and modernization is clearly present. If Madagascar fails to show an increased commitment to its structural reform, which for too long has followed a negative on-and-off cycle, then it would be difficult to justify increased donor support, particularly technical and financial support of policy reforms. In addition, the donor community must evaluate its own past performance — and the Bank is no exception — as a better-coordinated and better-designed program of assistance could have a more effective developmental impact.

CHAPTER 1

CAN MADAGASCAR REVERT FROM DECLINE TO HIGH GROWTH?

THE PROBLEM

1.1   Madagascar has become increasingly poorer over the last quarter century, with economic growth averaging a meager 0.5 percent a year and population growth rates averaging about 3 percent. Reflecting this decline, consumption per capita at 1997 prices has more than halved, from US$473 in 1970 to about US$227 in 1997. Wages of skilled workers have fallen in the same period from US$300 per month to US$50, and senior civil servants have seen their monthly pay decline from about US$900 a month in the early 1970s to close to US$170 in 1997. Poverty now affects three-quarters of the population, compared to about two-fifths at independence (see Box 1.1 for a brief description of Madagascar).

Table 1.1: Growth and GDP per Capita Performance for Countries which had in 1970 Incomes Similar to Madagascar

Country	Ratio of GDP per Capita to that of Madagascar 1970	Ratio of GDP per Capita to that of Madagascar 1995	Average Annual Growth Rate of GDP for 1970-95 (%)
Botswana	0.8	12.7	11.1
Korea	1.7	43.4	8.5
Indonesia	0.5	4.4	7.3
Lesotho	0.4	2.2	6.1
Pakistan	1.0	2.0	5.3
Tunisia	1.7	8.6	5.1
India	0.6	1.5	4.4
Madagascar	**1.0**	**1.0**	**0.5**

Source: World Bank Economic and Social Database and Africa Regional Database.

1.2   This disappointing economic performance is shocking in view of the many endowments and advantages of the country, and reflects past failed economic policies. Madagascar has adopted since independence an attitude not receptive of foreign investment, and one that allowed extensive State intervention in economic activities. Domestic and foreign investors have not been attracted to what is otherwise a resource-abundant economy, and allocation of resources has been distorted by excessive regulation. In contrast, other countries with income per capita in the early 1970s similar to that of Madagascar have performed much better by pursuing investment-friendly policies (see Table 1.1). The experience of other countries and Madagascar's wealth of resources suggest that, with policies supportive of a competitive private sector, the country can achieve the high growth rates that would enable convergence with these higher-income economies.

THE CHALLENGE

1.3   The absence of economic growth places Madagascar in a poverty trap. Policies that do not support investment hurt growth and, together with high population growth rates, result in falling per capita income. Low incomes result in low savings, and investment is thus insufficient to support economic development. In sum, physical and human capital are being consumed to the detriment of present and future generations. Madagascar's policies also are detrimental to foreign investment, precluding the country's access to new technologies and know-how. The challenge for policy makers is to break out of this vicious cycle, a task that requires defining a development strategy that highlights private sector growth and market competition.

Box 1.1: Madagascar at a Glance

Economy: Madagascar has an income per capita equivalent to about US$255, and a GDP of approximately US$3.6 billion. The structure of output is agriculture/primary activities, which account for 32 percent of GDP; industry, which accounts for 13 percent, with the food industry, energy, and the beverages industry as main sub-sectors; and services which accounts for about 55 percent.

Political System: The Constitution of 1998 established Madagascar as a decentralized State, and aims at facilitating the development of regions. As approved, the new constitution strengthens the role of the Presidency and establishes three elected levels of decentralized government.

Territory: Madagascar, located at the southeast of the African continent, has an area of 587,000 square kilometers and is by far the largest island in that region of the Indian Ocean. It has ample and varied resources, and a wide variety of soils and climates. Madagascar's environmental assets (flora and fauna) are unique in the world, but very much at risk as forests have been reduced. Main tourism attractions include the coasts in the northwest and the southeast.

Population: Madagascar's population was estimated at 14.1 million in mid-1997, and is growing at a 2.9 percent annual rate. Poverty afflicts 74 percent of the population, compared to about 40 percent in 1960. Life expectancy at birth is 52 years, and infant mortality rates are 90 per 1,000.

Relations with the World Bank/IDA: Madagascar became a member of the World Bank in 1963, three years after independence. IBRD and IDA have supported the development efforts of Madagascar since 1966. Assistance has included lending as well as non-lending services in the form of policy advice, economic and sector studies, and technical assistance. Financing has covered all main economic sectors, amounting to more than US$1.6 billion equivalent; about US$650 million in specific investment projects that have already been completed, US$550 million in investment projects under execution, and close to US$400 million in adjustment operations.

1.4   Undoubtedly, poverty is not only intimately related to Madagascar's lack of economic growth, but also to other factors such as wealth and income distribution. Poverty also manifests itself crudely through the many health, education, and housing deficiencies that affect large numbers of the Malagasy population. These manifestations are a reflection of what we have referred to as a poverty trap, but escaping from this trap requires putting in place the conditions that would enable attainment of high economic growth rates. High economic growth is by no means a sufficient condition to reduce Madagascar's extreme poverty, but is undoubtedly a necessary condition to achieve this goal.

Why is the Recent "African Growth Performance" not Good Enough for Madagascar?

1.5   Dramatic problems call for solutions out of the ordinary. The authorities should be aware that anything short of a complete reversal in performance would not significantly improve living standards. More specifically, a growth rate approximating the average of recent years in Sub-Saharan Africa — which is considered very good by many observers — would still fail to have a meaningful impact on Madagascar's poverty levels.

Table 1.2: Madagascar, Selected Projections under an
"African Performance Scenario," 1985-2015

	1985	1990	1995	1997	1998	2000	2005	2010	2015
GDP Growth (%)	1.2	3.1	1.7	3.6	3.9	4.5	4.5	4.5	4.5
Consumption per Capita in 1997 US$	297	251	228	227	229	229	232	255	286
Head-Count Index (% of pop. below poverty line)	59	68	73	74	74	74	73	69	63
As a percentage of GDP									
Gross Domestic Investment	8.5	14.8	10.9	11.8	12.8	13.8	16.5	16.6	16.6
Total Debt Outstanding	88	128	137	115	96	85	68	56	48
Foreign Direct Investment	0.0	0.5	0.2	0.4	0.5	0.9	1.0	0.8	0.8
In millions of US$									
Foreign Direct Investment	0	17	6	14	19	39	63	64	92

Note: Growth and investment match the average for 1994-97 in Sub-Saharan Africa.
Source: Staff estimates.

1.6   The arithmetic is simple and dramatically revealing. Growth rates increasing from current levels of about 3.5 percent — which are only slightly above the rate of population increase — to about 4.5 percent a year would represent a remarkable improvement relative to the country's performance since the early 1970s. These rates might be attained with a mix of the current responsible macroeconomic policies and less hesitant commitment to structural reforms, but with an economy essentially kept insular and over-regulated. Achieving this growth rate would also require an improvement in investment, from levels close to 12.5 percent of GDP in 1997 to about 16.5 percent by the middle of the next decade. This scenario would not help much the poor, however, since without a substantial change in external financing consumption expenditures would initially remain compressed at their current low levels, and would increase only gradually with higher growth. The population below the poverty line in Madagascar would remain above 70 percent before commencing a downward trend by the end of the next decade. This proportion would decrease to 64 percent by 2015 (see Table 1.2), assuming this relatively high growth — by Madagascar's standards — could continue within the framework of partial economic liberalization and openness, indeed in itself a strong assumption. Moreover, Madagascar would continue to rank high for illiteracy, poverty, and other negative indicators, and would continue to experience deteriorating health conditions, due mostly to communicable diseases.

What Economic Performance would Make a Sizable Dent in Poverty Levels?

1.7   Madagascar can introduce far-reaching reforms that would enable growth of about 7.5 percent a year without breaking the external financing constraint (see Table 1.3). High growth is also supported by many sectoral opportunities. For example, the tourism sector could more than double in size during the next 10 years, the export-manufacturing sector of the *zone franche* offers many possibilities, and vigorous development is expected in the mining sector. Two important projects already identified in the mining sector are in fact expected to bring in investments of US$900 million, and generate annual exports of about US$400 million by late next decade. The output from these three sectors would stimulate the rest of the economy. If this scenario were to materialize, consumption per capita could almost double in real terms by the year 2020, and poverty would decline to 32 percent in little more than 20 years, the lowest level in Madagascar's history (see Graph 1.1).

Graph 1.1: Poverty Level by 2020 under Different Growth Scenarios

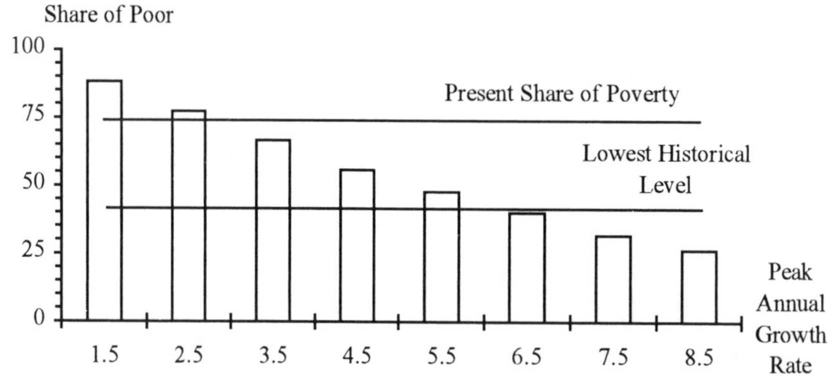

Source: World Bank estimates.

1.8   Is this feasible? We think so, although it must be recognized that the hurdles are high. In the short term, the implementation of an ambitious reform agenda would support higher growth by producing efficiency gains that will enable higher output levels for the same level of input. These reforms would also support a more efficient use of installed production capacity. To support medium- and long-term growth, however, Madagascar must encourage substantial savings. This is required to finance an expansion in essential public services and to sustain private investment at high levels. Total investment would need to gradually rise from slightly more than 12 percent of GDP in 1997 to about 20 percent by the year 2005, a level high by most African standards but at the low range of that of high-growth countries.

1.9   Increased public savings via higher taxes would provide an important contribution to higher national savings. Since the current level of non-interest government expenditures is low, amounting to about 17 percent of GDP, this suggests that — within a framework of better governance and increased efficiency — the public sector could expand without crowding out private investment. As discussed below, increased tax revenues will need to materialize through a broadening of the tax base and better tax administration, though efficiency gains in government expenditures are also necessary to reduce the likelihood of crowding-out effects. Within the appropriate policy environment and macro framework, private savings are likely to increase, thereby supporting necessary investments in different economic sectors.

Table 1.3: Madagascar, Economic Indicators, Actual Values and Projections under an Ambitious Reform Scenario, 1985-2015

	1997	1998	2000	2005	2010	2015
GDP Growth (%)	3.6	3.9	4.8	7.0	7.5	7.5
Consumption per Capita in 1997 US$	227	229	231	251	311	395
Head-Count Index (% of pop. below poverty line)	74	74	73	69	58	45
As a percentage of GDP						
Fiscal Deficit (before grants)	-7.7	-7.0	-6.4	-4.2	-3.0	-2.8
Fiscal Deficit (after grants)	-2.4	-2.1	-2.1	-1.3	-1.1	-1.6
Gross Domestic Investment	11.8	12.8	13.8	18.5	20.0	20.0
Total Debt Outstanding	115	94	81	58	43	38
Foreign Direct Investment	0.4	0.5	1.1	2.4	2.4	2.3
In millions of US$						
Foreign Direct Investment	14	19	47	160	259	383

Source: Staff estimates.

THE PROPOSED STRATEGY AND THE REFORM AGENDA

1.10   What is necessary to achieve an impressive mobilization of resources, an increase in per capita consumption, and a reduction of poverty? Two elements are crucial, and this report is devoted to discussing them in detail. These are:

- mechanisms and policies to foster private sector growth within a competitive market framework (discussed in Chapter 2); and

- a reform program to redefine the role of the public sector, supporting private sector development while increasing the quality and quantity of public services (Chapter 3).

Related to both of these policy areas, it is clear that greater openness to the outside world is a necessary condition for high growth and private sector development. This is required so that in the short and medium terms Madagascar can register both increases in consumption and increases in investment. More generally, foreign investment will go a long way in improving the efficiency of the economy by supplying know-how and modern technologies. In addition, the mining sector is likely to develop only with substantial foreign investment and participation. A similar argument applies to other economic sectors.

Fostering Private Sector Development

1.11   The dramatic increase in output described before can ultimately occur only if the private sector develops. It is therefore of crucial importance to remove the constraints that make Madagascar a bad place to do business, both for domestic and foreign entrepreneurs. The growth agenda for Madagascar requires measures that rapidly restore investor confidence and facilitate the flow of investment. While Madagascar has gradually begun to introduce the framework and pre-conditions that support high growth, the scenario proposed in this report requires an even greater commitment to reform.

1.12   The credibility of the legal system must be strengthened and property rights and contracts must be respected to support high investment and growth. In the long term, the entire judicial system must be strengthened, but allowing for international arbitration of commercial disputes may be worth considering as a short-term solution.

1.13   Fostering an enabling business environment also implies moving from a paternalistic State that dispenses favors and protects the private sector from competition, to a more liberal economic policy environment that supports competitive markets. The most immediate need is to limit discretionary actions and to simplify administrative procedures to reduce the likelihood of these ad hoc, non-transparent actions. For example, standard operating procedures should be modified to create a level playing field for all investors, and to provide needed authorizations in a quasi-automatic, time-bound manner.

1.14   Implementing a privatization strategy that induces competitive and ownership behaviors is another main component of the proposed strategy. Privatization serves to improve the operational efficiency of viable public enterprises by spinning them off to experienced, autonomous, and risk-taking entrepreneurs. Foreign expertise is required in many sectors, but mechanisms to facilitate local ownership have been appropriately envisaged in Madagascar's privatization strategy. The rapid and transparent implementation of this strategy will signal to investors a decisive break with past policies and behavior, and is something that Madagascar must convincingly put in evidence. In sum, the government must develop its role as facilitator of the private sector, and adopt an attitude aimed at addressing the constraints faced by investors.

Redefining the Role of the State

1.15   In addition to an ambitious privatization agenda that will serve to signal a clear break with the past and the end of direct State intervention in economic activities, public finances must be redefined. Total revenues without grants have markedly fallen during the 1990s, and need to increase to about 17 percent of GDP in the next 10 years, from about 9.5 percent in 1997. This will require decisive action to address mostly tax-base and tax-administration issues, as the tax structure in Madagascar is relatively modern and well designed. Non-tax revenues also need to play a more important role, particularly mining and fishing rights. These concessions and licenses are not transparently allocated, and the fees being channeled to Treasury accounts are very low by international standards.

1.16   Public expenditure levels are low in comparison to other Sub-Saharan countries, and need to be increased to provide needed public goods and services. Primary education and vocational training are important and should be emphasized, together with increased primary health care. As a comparison, Madagascar spends US$4 per capita on public health, and US$8 on education, about half the recommended average for low-income countries (World Bank, World Development Report, 1993).

1.17   Increased expenditures should not be made without first increasing government efficiency, however. A sensible strategy must be developed that addresses not only the low levels of expenditures, but also, and perhaps above all, the effective delivery of these expenditures. If weaknesses in this area are not eliminated, the likelihood is high that the impact of increased public sector expenditures would be minimal or even detrimental for investment and growth.

1.18   For increased revenue collection not to be wasted, therefore, the public sector must first significantly increase its efficiency. This requires many institutional and organizational changes. Establishing a more transparent administration of public finances and greater budgetary discipline rank high among the tasks that lie ahead, and are necessary not only to finance more expenditure in social sectors, but also as a signal of change and political modernization. A more sensible organization of the civil service must be made such that the proportion of public servants directly serving the Malagasy population is increased. In this respect, decentralizing government services is also important, as this will serve to better match needs and resources and thereby ensure increased delivery effectiveness.

Opening Up the Economy

1.19   Opening up the economy is also a necessity, not only to support the two areas of action described above, but also for financial and technological reasons. Arithmetic again suggests that Madagascar would be well served by providing opportunities for increased FDI flow. FDI provides technology and non-debt creating financing, but can also help Madagascar break out of the vicious cycle of poverty by reinforcing growth and allowing both consumption and investment to rise, by invigorating the economy through the adoption of international best practices, and by unleashing the country's potential in key economic sectors (see Box 1.2). Madagascar's FDI levels are dismal, and compare with those of countries that have seen the ravages of war and famine. The challenge for Madagascar is to gradually and convincingly attract more FDI, which potentially can rise from US$14 million in 1997 to about US$160 million by 2005 and to more than US$380 million by 2015. An additional advantage worth noting is that high growth and large levels of FDI would allow Madagascar to embark on a development path on which debt indicators adopt a rapidly declining trend. If the country achieved the levels of FDI indicated, total debt would decline from about 100 percent of GDP to less than 40 percent by 2015 (see Table 1.3). The concessional terms of Madagascar's external debt and the debt relief provided by the donor community would support this decline.

Box 1.2: The High Costs of a Strategy without Foreign Direct Investment

Any one of the factors needed for growth — the upgrade and increase of human capital, an increase in the stock of capital and its efficient use, policies that support competition, and so on — could trigger Madagascar's breakout from the poverty trap. In turn, these factors could be financed through larger domestic savings, expanding borrowing from abroad, increasing FDI, or eliciting donor support. However, borrowing is not an option in view of heavy indebtedness, and though higher domestic savings will need to be achieved, this will be to the detriment of consumption per capita.

Eliciting a quantum leap in FDI, together with donor support, is necessary to enable an increase in per capita consumption and in investment, particularly in the short-term before high growth materializes. Alternatively, the government could aim at further reducing consumption to reach the same investment level and, in turn, the same growth path; implicitly assuming that sufficient domestic savings will be mobilized and that efficiency is constant. This is a very strong assumption, however, since an enabling business environment must be conducive to, and will benefit from, increased FDI levels. If the economy does not open up, then it is likely that equal levels of investment would be insufficient to achieve high growth (i.e., efficiency is likely to be much lower).

If the country opens up to foreign investment and mobilizes donor support for its growth strategy, consumption per capita would rise by the end of the scenario period and poverty would decline to 69 percent by 2005, 58 percent by 2010, and 45 percent by 2015. Alternatively, in the absence of a quantum leap in FDI, the poverty head-count index will decline less in the initial years. Is higher poverty the only cost of a development strategy without foreign direct investment? The answer is, once again, a conclusive no. A strategy that does not attract FDI would suggest that reform commitment is limited, and that an enabling business environment is not being aggressively pursued; growth would therefore be much lower. Notwithstanding the above, it is worth highlighting that Madagascar in the high-growth scenario of this report would, by 2015, be investing about 20 percent of GDP, of which only 2.3 percent of GDP is financed through foreign direct investment.

1.20   Are there any alternatives? In addition to efficiency gains, increases in total factor productivity can be achieved either by buying know-how and technology (the South Korean model) or by acquiring it through foreign investment (the Hong Kong model). But Madagascar's debt burden precludes increased borrowing from abroad as a way of acquiring technology, so the Hong Kong model of financing may be the only option. Foreign direct investment also has the added advantage of providing access to new geographical and product markets, and has been linked to positive spill-over effects across the economy through, among other, its impact on developing managerial skills. Moreover, it must not be forgotten that aid is no replacement for the stimulating effect of an increased flow of foreign private capital.

1.21   Is an increased reliance on FDI realistic? The answer is yes. International experience shows that FDI flows of between 1.5 and 5 percent of GDP are possible among a diverse group of countries (see Table 1.4), but only if the government creates a favorable business environment. Several countries have been able to attract FDI in recent years despite having none in 1990, mainly by adopting policies conducive to macroeconomic sustainability and supportive of private sector development. The scenario target of US$160 million of FDI a year within 10 years is feasible, since it amounts to an average of about 2.4 percent of GDP. Continuous inflows of capital would require further economic liberalization to develop efficient markets and increased emphasis on education, as a trained and educated labor force is a significant factor governing the choice of host country made by foreign investors (see Box 1.3 and the annex to this report for an evaluation of Madagascar's economic performance during the last 10 years).

Table 1.4: Foreign Direct Investment in Selected Countries
(net FDI in millions of US$ and growth rates in percentages)

Countries	Net FDI 1990	Net FDI 1995	FDI/GDP 1990	FDI/GDP 1995	GDP Growth 1990-95 (%)
Cape Verde	-0.1	3	0.0%	0.9%	3.9
Peru	41	2326	0.1%	4.1%	4.2
Uganda	6	113	0.1%	1.9%	6.8
Sri Lanka	43	158	0.5%	1.2%	4.8
Morocco	165	824	0.6%	2.5%	1.7
Mozambique	9	35	0.6%	2.4%	5.7
Laos	6	77	0.7%	4.4%	6.5
China	2657	30987	0.8%	4.7%	10.9

Source: World Bank Economic and Social Database and Africa Regional Database.

1.22   Experience also indicates that investors take two to four years to respond to policy reforms. Madagascar could elicit a faster reaction, however, because many potential private sector investment decisions have been delayed due to the lukewarm commitment of the government to private sector development. Paradoxically, Madagascar could benefit from its past hesitancy by clearly signaling a break from its past attitudes. While this report proposes increased FDI as a means of achieving growth and increases in per capita consumption, however, it is worth highlighting that of the total gross investment of 20 percent of GDP calculated for 2015, only 2.3 percentage points would be financed through FDI.

1.23   Madagascar must also show a positive attitude toward visitors from abroad, the benefits of which extend beyond the development of the tourism sector. In this regard, the visa changes introduced in 1997 are a welcome event, which together with partial air transport liberalization have resulted in an increase in the number of tourists arriving in Madagascar of about 35 percent. Foreign exchange earnings from the tourism sector peaked in 1997 at about US$60 million, 28 percent more than the previous year.

Box 1.3: Lessons from Madagascar's Past Economic Policies

Madagascar first undertook structural adjustment in the mid-1980s after several attempts at socialist-type policies. The program was supported by both the World Bank and the IMF, and resulted in significant policy gains that led to a three-year period of economic growth (1988-90). Policy gains were made in the following areas: (i) an automatic allocation mechanism of foreign exchange was introduced; (ii) export restrictions were abolished for all products except vanilla; (iii) two private banks were authorized to begin operations; (iv) 50 public enterprises were privatized; and (v) liberalization of the oil and telecommunications sectors began. Implementation of the reform agenda progressed, and per capita incomes stabilized after many years of continued decline. Unfortunately, mismanagement of aggregate demand, together with external shocks, soon led to a devaluation.

In July 1992, a transition government was appointed. This government allowed budgetary discipline to deteriorate, let slide monetary management, replaced the automatic allocation of foreign exchange with rationing instruments, and interrupted the privatization process. In sum, Madagascar returned to the failed economic policies of the past.

A new National Assembly was elected in August 1993. After some initial setbacks in economic policy making, including the imposition of import restrictions, the government resumed its adjustment efforts by (i) floating the currency, and (ii) abolishing import prohibitions. The government also signed a Policy Framework Paper with the Bretton Woods institutions in 1994. This period provided the basis for recovery, much of which was strengthened by reforms initiated in 1996.

Madagascar is now at a turning point. Opening up the economy, supporting private sector development, and redefining the role of the State are key elements to achieve growth and reduce poverty, as proven by the country's timid reform attempts of the recent past. Its emphasis on economic self-sufficiency and nationalism have not only prevented Madagascar from learning from the enriching experiences of countries all over the world, but have also resulted in inefficient allocation of resources, particularly now that world markets are increasingly integrated.

1.24   Is increased donor assistance an alternative? Concessional aid will be needed, particularly since investor response will only gradually materialize in increased FDI levels. Without this assistance it will be difficult to increase investment in human capital and physical infrastructure to levels compatible with rapid development. About US$200 million annually of official grant assistance will be required — slightly more than 40 percent more than in our scenario envisaging growth rates of 4.5 percent a year, but the same level reached in 1997. To justify such exceptional financial support from bilateral and multilateral sources, the implementation of bold structural reforms and the opening up of the economy should be sustained. An important caveat must, however, be raised. The low absorptive capacity of the country is a major constraint to increased aid disbursements, and the government's counterpart funds might be difficult to deliver. Many of the changes suggested to redefine the role of the State are therefore important if sustained high levels of donor financing are to have an impact on growth.

Conclusion

1.25   For Madagascar to achieve its economic potential, those economic sectors and individuals that have benefited from years of protection and special favors need to be confronted with the challenge of increased competition. The country should open up the economy to investors, domestic and foreign, without recourse to special favors or schemes that may limit competition. Undoubtedly, the strategy proposed in this report is ambitious, and political will and conviction are required for it to materialize, but the benefits would soon extend to all of the Malagasy population as new economic activities develop, employment expands, and incomes rise. This strategy is also supported by promising sectoral opportunities that have remained dormant for more than three decades, and that could show rapid growth in a framework of government commitment to reform. Mining and tourism are two of these key sectors.

1.26   The rest of this report explores the stance that the government needs to take in support of growth. Chapter 2 discusses the stimulation of private sector growth, and Chapter 3 the redefinition of the role of the public sector. The aim is to establish how the described areas of action would underpin the proposed growth strategy. Both areas would require an economy that is more open to foreign investors and visitors, as has been the experience of other high-growth countries.

HOW TO UNLEASH PRIVATE SECTOR DEVELOPMENT?

2.1   Madagascar could meet the ambitious growth targets discussed in Chapter 1 by removing existing constraints on investors, particularly in the mining and tourism sectors but also in many other service sectors. Cross-country evidence suggests that success will require credible reforms to stabilize and liberalize the economy, and effective policies to increase the depth of the financial sector, including cleaning up portfolio problems. Substantial progress has been achieved in all of these areas, and much more is expected in 1998, with the privatization of the two remaining publicly-owned banks and the preparation for privatization of the key non-banking financial institutions, the state-owned insurance companies Ny Havana and Aro.

2.2   The government must also complement the progress achieved in macroeconomic stabilization, economic liberalization, and financial-sector restructuring with (i) the pursuit of policies aimed at privatizing state-owned enterprises, (ii) the creation of a legal environment conducive to private sector development, (iii) the reduction of administrative barriers to investment, and (iv) the liberalization of key economic sectors. Sector-specific institutional bottlenecks blocking development must also be addressed. The aim of this chapter is to examine these policies.

PRIVATIZATION

2.3   Madagascar has more than 120 public enterprises with important roles in agriculture, mining, utilities, air, sea and rail transport, infrastructure, and the financial sector. The public sector accounts for about one-third of output, half of modern sector employment, more than half of total investment, and about 40 percent of domestic credit. Even in the absence of explicit subsidies, most public enterprises are a financial burden through their failure to repay the full value of loans from the government and/or their potential tax obligations. The high cost of public enterprises is most dramatically demonstrated by the two state-owned commercial banks, for which the Malagasy population now faces a bill of about US$80 million.

2.4   More importantly, government intervention in productive activities and commercial services restricts competition and distorts resource allocation, negatively affecting economic growth. For example, the transport sector, broadly defined, comprises only public enterprises, including Air Madagascar, SOFITRANS, ADEMA, AUXIMAD, SMTM, and CMN. The entry of competing operators is restricted, and relative prices thereby distorted.

2.5   Privatization is a key element of Madagascar's private sector growth strategy (see Box 2.1) and should improve the operational efficiency of public enterprises (PEs) by spinning them off to experienced, autonomous, and risk-taking entrepreneurs. Privatization should also enable the government to reduce the fiscal burden of inefficient PEs that do not pay their taxes or debts to the state, and, above all, should send a clear signal of a break with the past. This will help to mobilize domestic and foreign investors, while reducing the costs across all economic sectors through the provision of more efficient and less expensive services, such as telecoms and transport.

Box 2.1: How to Mitigate the Social Consequences of Privatization

Ownership is a significant determinant of enterprise performance. All over the world, good public enterprise performance has been difficult to bring about and, when achieved, hard to sustain. These difficulties drive privatization around the world. While much of the emphasis is on the potential fiscal burden, the real reason to pursue privatization is its impact in improving efficiency across all economic sectors and in restoring investor confidence. In sum, privatization with competition yields substantial and enduring benefits: lower prices and better service; higher wages reflecting higher productivity; faster growth; and better capital structures.

Privatization is often initially accompanied by layoffs, but over time, as the firm and the economy embark on a high-growth path, the trend is reversed. In fact, many divested firms in the Philippines, Tunisia, Mexico, and Chile have in the medium-term increased net employment. The temporary effects of unemployment must nonetheless be addressed. Significant success has been observed in countries that have established re-training programs. In some cases, personnel whose services are not required are likely to be offered the option of a monthly payment for a fixed number of months, or a large single payment at the time of layoff. The latter method has been successfully used in many countries, particularly Central and Eastern European and Latin American countries. Its attractiveness lies in that it helps to develop small entrepreneurial undertakings that would otherwise not be possible, due to the lack of access to initial capital.

2.6   However, to be effective, the government must act decisively by: (i) ensuring the transparency of the privatization process through the use of clear guidelines and procedures that reduce the possibilities for abuse; (ii) allowing open and equal access for all potential and qualified investors, encouraging local ownership but without discouraging the foreign investment which that is needed to modernize the capital and management structures of privatized firms; and (iii) aggressively pursuing privatization in sectors such as air transport, telecoms, and petroleum, introducing regulatory frameworks that would increase competition and prevent private monopoly rents.

2.7   Encouraging local private investment in the PEs to be privatized is an important component of any successful privatization strategy. It helps support growth of domestic savings and the development of local capital markets. It also helps foster popular understanding and support for the privatization process. However, there are trade-offs between improving efficiency and maximizing local participation. First, local savings are thin and managerial capabilities weak. Foreign investors can bring in expertise and strategic market links, and may be the only source of the investment capital needed to re-orient and modernize these enterprises. Second, over-emphasis on domestic ownership can slow down privatization and diminish efficiency gains. Finally, equitable treatment of foreign and domestic private capital will help to build investor confidence, with positive implications for attracting FDI.

Different mechanisms to promote domestic participation have been successfully used in a number of developing countries. One successful mechanism used elsewhere has been to sell a *strategic* and *controlling* interest to the foreign companies that bring the necessary expertise and investment capital, while maintaining a minority share under government ownership. The government does not intervene in the day-to-day operations and, through different mechanisms, gradually sells to local investors its remaining equity participation. A discussion of the mechanisms chosen by Madagascar is presented in Box 2.2.

Box 2.2: Mechanisms to Promote Local Ownership and Distribute Privatization Proceeds

Madagascar's privatization process is regulated by the Loi 96-011 enacted in August of 1996. The sole exceptions are the State disengagement from the two remaining public banks, BTM and BFV, the privatization of which had already begun. The government has announced a list of 45 firms from which it plans to divest its interest by end-1999, and additional lists are expected to follow. The process has thus far evolved slowly, with only the initial preparatory work being completed. With the intention of facilitating participation of the Malagasy population in the privatization process, the law establishes two funds:

• **Privatization Fund**. This fund, administered temporarily by a specially created State organization, is allowed to hold a minority share of each privatized enterprise. The organization is then tasked with selling its stake in privatized firms to workers in the privatized firms, to Malagasy citizens, and to enterprise and financial institutions with majority ownership by Malagasy nationals. Other options for local participation were considered, but the government viewed the proposed system as more attractive since no contributions from individuals are required at the time of privatization, enabling the delay of local participation without affecting the privatization schedule.

• **Social and Regional Development Fund**. The social fund aims to direct the net proceeds from the privatization process to those sectors of the population that are most in need of assistance, and to channel resources to regional development activities. To do so, the fund will direct privatization resources to activities developing infrastructure and strengthening the microfinance institutions that will help improve the living conditions of those that are unable to become direct participants in privatized firms.

2.8   The government's commitment to the privatization process will be evidenced by how rapidly and decisively the divestiture from key enterprises and sectors takes place, which will in turn signal to investors a decisive break with past policies and behavior. This applies specifically to those enterprises that have significant market power, such as Air Madagascar, SOLIMA (involved mostly in the distribution of petroleum products), TELMA (telecoms), and JIRAMA (power and water). Other countries that have adopted ambitious privatization strategies in similar sectors have seen a spurt in domestic and foreign investment across all economic sectors, because of the influence of service sector enterprises on other enterprises and economic activities. High prices and poor service increase the costs of what otherwise would seem completely unrelated activities. In the case of Madagascar, for example, obtaining a fixed telephone line may take many years, and the air transport sector still has marked oligopolistic price-setting features. With World Bank support, the government designed and implemented reforms in 1997 enabling the establishment of cellular communications operators, and increased access to the air transport market by authorizing additional regular airline and charter operators. Prices have consequently decreased and service has improved, contributing to a 35 percent increase in the number of tourists during 1997.

CREATING A FAVORABLE LEGAL ENVIRONMENT

2.9   The legal environment of Madagascar is typical of many developing countries. As reflected in an assessment by the 1996 International Business Law Journal, the legal framework of LDCs deters international investors, and local economic agents operate in the context of informal structures which emerge as a result of the prevailing legal and judicial insecurity. Increased transparency is critical particularly in the key economic sectors awaiting the design and implementation of sector specific regulatory frameworks.

2.10   The weaknesses of Madagascar's legal environment can be grouped under five main headings. First, a series of outdated legal texts has combined with recent updates to create a peculiar mix of French law and Malagasy custom. For example, the law concerning *sociétés anonymes* dates back to 1867, and that on limited liability companies to 1925 (for a thorough discussion, see Etude sur la Gouvernance, UNDP, 1997). Second, access to legal texts and related legal documentation is limited by lack of means — judges often lack key legal documentation, including relevant decrees, and as a result cannot effectively carry out their duties, for example. Third, clearly established property rights do not exist, with land tenure standing out as a main development constraint that Malagasy society needs to address without delay. Fourth, an arbitration system for resolving commercial disputes is not in place. If developed, this could help to gradually restore investor confidence. Finally, training for magistrates and clerks has until recently lagged, the judicial infrastructure is in poor condition, and the pay of magistrates is far from sufficient to compensate for their responsibilities. Undoubtedly, improvements in these areas would facilitate the development of Madagascar's economy. In a similar case, the police force must be provided with the means necessary to strengthen public security.

2.11   In order to streamline the legislative reform process, the government established in January 1996 a Business Law Reform Commission, which has primary responsibility for the supervision of the revision of business law. Despite some progress on the Concurrence Law, on the bank credits recovery, and on liberalizing how interest rates are set, the commission has not worked regularly and effectively. It may be necessary to streamline the procedures of the commission, and to establish a timetable for action on the work program that has been defined. The following paragraphs discuss in more detail the five main weaknesses of Madagascar's legal environment, Bank assistance in these areas, and what remains to be done to improve the judicial system.

2.12   **Outdated Legislation**. French law was formally introduced into Madagascar in 1895. In the absence of applicable provisions in the modern law, however, Malagasy courts still apply customary-law principles to the extent they are ascertainable, well-established, and not contrary to public order or good practices. However, the complex interaction between French and Malagasy law makes their application very difficult. It is necessary for the Business Legal Reform Commission to quickly complete the work on legislative reform. This will bring greater certainty to the existing legal foundation, and to additional weaknesses yet to be addressed.

2.13   **Access to Legal Documentation**. Improving access to codes and legal documentation is a key element in the restoration of confidence in the judicial system. The World Bank has envisaged providing support in two distinct activities: the publication of laws, and the publication of a legal journal. The compilation and the publication of laws is expected to be completed before the end of 1998. Commercial and business laws will be published as a complete set, and will become readily available to judges, magistrates, lawyers, and other interested parties. The Bank is currently financing local consulting services for the preparation of technological tools for establishing and managing a legal information system at the Ministry of Justice.

2.14   **Property Rights**. Title ownership is recognized under Malagasy law. The rights of foreigners to own immovable property in Madagascar has been severely restricted, however, making it virtually impossible to have access to this type of property. The sole legal alternative is the so-called *bail emphytéotique*, a mechanism through which land may be leased for a period of 99 years. Unfortunately, this is not always an available option, as most land is owned by the government but its allocation regulated by existing land tenure rights, which take into consideration customary rules. A Bank-financed study has suggested that the long-term lease needs to be modified so that investors would be able to obtain leases with delays shorter to those that currently exist, and through the use of non-discretionary and clear criteria for the assessment of lease applications. As discussed in the next section, however, the subject of land tenure extends beyond nationality.

2.15   **Arbitration for Resolving Commercial Disputes**. Arbitration systems offer a unique opportunity to resolve commercial disputes, enabling circumvention of the slow Malagasy judicial system and providing the possibility of faster and more equitable solutions. The implementation of arbitration procedures in Madagascar faces three problems. First, the specific legal texts have to be updated, as the official texts date from the last century. Second, the implementation of arbitration rules is inadequate, as although perceptions vary significantly between regions, Malagasy magistrates do not in general accept arbitration procedures. Finally, arbitration rules are not very well known, with the exception of in the city and main international harbor of Toamasina, and are considered a parallel justice process to be often reconsidered for validation by a tribunal when one party contests the arbitration result. The Bank undertook a study in August 1997 to evaluate different mechanisms for improving commercial arbitration procedures, and a proposal for a new arbitration law was prepared in October 1997. The new legislation establishes that the parties of a contract may agree to incorporate the arbitration clause. Once they do, they are bound by any future arbitration decision. This draft legislation must now be submitted for approval to the National Assembly.

2.16   **Institutional and Structural Deficiencies**. A good legal environment requires magistrates trained in the administration of a modern judicial system and compensated in accordance with their responsibilities. Salary levels in Madagascar range from US$40 a month for junior magistrates to about US$120 for a few of their most senior colleagues. Good training and equitable salaries are particularly important if lack of transparency in the administration of justice is to be eliminated or even reduced from its currently worrisome levels. An *Ecole Nationale de la Magistrature et des Greffes* (ENMG) was created at the end of 1996 with World Bank assistance. This school aims at providing training to judges and other personnel of the judicial system, and has provided training to more than two-thirds of Madagascar's magistrates since January 1997. Two priority actions still remain to be considered: the first is to strengthen the ENMG in its pedagogical program and financial situation to ensure regular training at national and international levels; the second is to assure the sustainability of this new institution. This will be achieved partly through the appointment of a pedagogical specialist to ensure continuity in training programs.

2.17   A number of factors, most of which are budget-related, have combined to undermine the effectiveness of judges and magistrates and to reduce confidence in the justice system. These range from poor salaries to lack of proper facilities and equipment, and to inadequate provision of library facilities. The Bank undertook a study in August 1997 for a new incentives pay system that seeks to improve the productivity of magistrates. In addition, during the recent Public Expenditure Review mission, the donors suggested increases in budget appropriations for the Ministry of Justice to cover wage bill and performance indemnities, goods and services, and public investment for infrastructure rehabilitation. These were approved by the authorities in the 1998 budget law. The Bank will also finance some reconstitution and expansion of library facilities and documentation, and the publication of revised editions of existing laws.

2.18   In sum, much remains to be done in the sphere of legal reform. The strategy of the government should be to clarify the laws and decrees by which the private sector should abide and to strengthen enforcement of these laws. Increased transparency is also critical in those key economic sectors that are awaiting the design and implementation of sector specific regulatory and legal frameworks. In the short term, and before these reforms are implemented, it is imperative that the government consider bolder solutions that could have positive and immediate impact on growth. Pending additional reform of the legal system over the medium term, developing the necessary regulations for implementing an effective arbitration system for resolving commercial disputes is worth considering.

REDUCING ADMINISTRATIVE AND REGULATORY BARRIERS TO INVESTMENT

2.19   In addition to the legal issues discussed above, the business community perceives the Malagasy government as not supportive of private sector development. The State has a role in providing authorizations and enforcing regulations, but it is also responsible for exercising this right with balance and for not abusing it by imposing unwarranted delays or introducing ad hoc decision-making mechanisms. Three areas are worth highlighting to facilitate investment:

removing entry barriers; eliminating regulations that discourage bankruptcy procedures and other exit costs; and addressing land tenure issues that negatively affect investment decisions.

2.20   **Entry Barriers**. Potential investors, domestic and foreign, face high transaction costs and long waiting periods due to excessive bureaucratic formalities. Lack of information about the different formalities to be met also leads to delays. Direct and indirect fixed costs associated with registrations, licenses, and permits can represent an important investment burden, penalizing all but the largest investors. The existing web of required permits is so cumbersome that a service industry has developed to help firms navigate the maze of regulations for setting up a company. The fact that there are so many entities involved in the registration process also presents fertile ground for corruption. In addition to the direct costs of firm registration, the time involved in this process is long and unpredictable. For example, unless a company seeks the help of investment "facilitators," it takes at least 35 days to set up a Société à Responsabilité Limitée, 50 days to set up a Société Anonyme, and more than six months to set up an export processing zone company.

2.21   To support private sector development, the government should aim at simplifying the existing rules, which are unnecessarily complicated and time-consuming. One possible way of simplifying the process would be to aim at imposing on government departments a time limit for action, after which the authorizations can be considered to have been made. This system of automaticity has been effectively used in many other countries, and the government should consider the introduction of a similar mechanism here. For example, authorizations could be automatically issued after a statutory period of one month; if necessary, with a one-month extension. Administrative regulations that could be treated this way include legalization and registration of statutes, and the regulations through which companies are registered. In addition, administrative procedures for foreign investment must be simplified. The latter should draw on the best practices of countries that are successful in attracting foreign investment, such as Cape Verde and Ghana.

2.22   The government could also consider creating an investment promotion agency that would be assigned the task of identifying the legal and regulatory bottlenecks faced by potential private sector investors, domestic or foreign, and develop proposals to address these deficiencies. Much of its work could develop from simply hearing from investors what are the main constraints they face. In addition, the agency could have an informational and promotional role in clarifying the rules and laws to which the private sector must abide, and could complement this role with activities that promote investment in Madagascar. The agency should, however, have no role in providing the authorizations required by any specific investor. This has been proven in the past to lead to increased corruption, which in turn negatively affects economic growth.

2.23   **Exit Costs**. Few, if any, bankruptcy cases reach their conclusion, notwithstanding Article 511 of the Commercial Code, which requires bankruptcies to be settled within three months. Bankruptcy procedures are long, costly, and unclear, as is the rest of the judicial system. The main obstacles are labor indemnization costs, and inefficient and corrupt court officials. It is difficult for a company to stop its operations, and exit by selling assets is complicated by excessive regulations, particularly those that limit foreign ownership of land. These barriers deter private sector development, because in market economies the bankruptcy procedure is the mechanism through which economic resources are redirected to more efficient use. The government should evaluate ways to facilitate the use of the bankruptcy framework.

2.24   **Land Access**. Access to land and real estate is also an important constraint for investors, with the debate often wrongly seen as a problem of ownership of land by foreigners (see Box 2.3). The real problem is that land ownership rights are unclear, both for domestic and for foreign investors. About 80 percent of the land is supposed to be public land owned by the State (*domaine privé de l'état*), and only about 10 percent of the total land area is covered by legal title. In practice, most land is occupied and used on the basis of customary allocations.

Box 2.3: Access of Foreign Investors to Land

Traditional attachment to ancestral lands is deeply rooted in Malagasy society. As a result, access to land by foreigners has been an issue of controversy and considerable cultural sensitivity. In practice, foreign investors pay for using the name of Malagasy nationals to purchase real estate: this does nothing to eliminate the uncertainty over property rights, and also negatively affects the business environment within which the private sector operates.

The access of local and foreign investors to land has on paper been eased with the establishment of the *bail emphytéotique*, which allows leases to be transferable, mortgageable and renewable. Two types of land can be leased: (i) private lands belonging to private persons, where formalities for an *emphytéotique* lease are straightforward; and (ii) public lands belonging to the State, with a long waiting period for the leasing procedures to be completed. Delays are usually more than six months, with a median of about three years — even though current procedures of the Ministry of Town and Country Planning stipulate the process be completed in 60 working days.

Several studies have been done on how to simplify and speed up access to public land. These suggest, for example, that the government should instruct government departments to undertake various authorization procedures simultaneously rather than consecutively; that they should set up permanent committees to consider applications; and that they should involve local communities early on in the decision-making process.

2.25   The lack of legal title is a hurdle to borrowing from banks, and therefore inhibits long-term investment. The absence of title is also a constraint to the use of land as a tax base, and mechanisms to rapidly address this deficiency should be sought. As an example, with support from the World Bank and the Australian government, Thailand has nearly completed its national land titling and valuation program, providing secure title to the land of virtually every farmer in the country and an important source of tax revenues to the government. Similarly, Indonesia and Laos are implementing their own 25-year national titling programs. Benefits from a secure title, as compared to untitled land, are: (i) increased access to institutional credit and decreased reliance on informal credit sources; (ii) an incentive for more frequent use of inputs such as fertilizers; and (iii) increased investments in land, including land improvements. The government should also provide adequate financial resources to an interministry committee in charge of studies aimed at simplifying procedures, developing a participatory process that engages the different local communities, improving the quality of service of the land tenure services, and supporting the institutions engaged in land tenure issues.

2.26   In addition to making leases easier and faster to obtain, bolder, innovative solutions are required. The government could combine a land-titling program with giving local governments responsibility over land. More specifically, and given the importance of local customary use of land, the central government may wish to devolve decision-making authority on this subject to local governments, with a right of appeal to central government venues.

2.27   The government could additionally allocate large tracts of public land for development, and instruct the relevant government departments to complete all formalities for transfer of these tracts of land. Emergency measures to provide access to land are particularly urgent for tourism development and industrial parks. To accommodate an average of between 10 and 15 percent additional tourists each year, domestic and foreign investors will need to expand hotel infrastructure. Since the applicants will by and large be internationally established hotel chains, government must ensure that attractive sites are made available. To accomplish this goal, the government could locate and delimit special tourist zones and give its own guarantees against interference by any third party and competing property claims, even those originating in local governments. Transfers of land title could thereby be effected immediately. Tourism is essential for growth. As discussed in the next section, receipts from tourism, which amounted to US$58 million in 1997, could significantly increase within an investor-friendly environment.

2.28   It must be emphasized that a solution to Madagascar's land tenure issues can only develop from a process that matures within Malagasy civil society. The discussion above aims only to stimulate constructive dialogue, as there is widespread agreement that this is a major stumbling block to Madagascar's economic development. The World Bank view on this subject is two fold. In the short term, we believe the country may benefit from interim solutions such as those described above, be they the development of industrial and tourism zones, a more effective and transparent application of the so-called *bail emphytéotique*, or a combination of these and other land-access policies. In the long term, however, a more lasting and efficient solution is required, and it is Madagascar's population and civil society that must come up with this solution.

ECONOMIC POTENTIAL IN THE AGRICULTURAL, MINING AND TOURISM SECTORS

2.29   Madagascar is a resource-abundant country with great economic potential. Agricultural production and mining activities are two key economic sectors. However, due in part to excessive State intervention, the development prospects of these sectors has been lagging. Similarly, policies of economic isolationism have led to an environment not supportive of the tourism sector. The aim of this section is to highlight the lessons derived from excessive government intervention in agriculture and mining, and to examine what remains to be done to liberalize these economic activities. Economic development in these sectors is also affected by institutional and organizational factors, such as the regulatory framework for mining activities and the policies to support the dissemination of technology and know-how to the agricultural sector. The section also discusses the potential of the tourism sector, together with the main developmental bottlenecks that need to be addressed.

2.30   **Agriculture**. There are many different kinds of distortions in the agricultural sector. For example, through its many different parastatals the government still holds a monopoly of cotton and sugar marketing, as well as production activities in some of these sectors. These parastatals administer farm-gate prices at below international levels. Also, farmers are exposed to low producer prices due to the existence of trading cartels, particularly among export crops. Donor fertilizer grants have been sold in the past at subsidized prices through favored enterprises, preventing the development of a fertilizer market and resulting in low utilization levels relative to the experience of other countries. This is particularly true in the rice sector. Airfreight costs to and from Madagascar are about 40 percent higher than in neighboring Mauritius, and this discourages growth of non-traditional exports such as flowers. Finally, the costs of maritime freight are exorbitant, because of the inefficiency of port operations at Toamasina.

Table 2.1: Madagascar, Agriculture Potential, Target Yields for the Next Decade

PRODUCTS	Rice Paddy	Manioc	Vanilla	Coffee	Sugar Cane	Maize	Cotton	Peanuts	TOTAL
Current Prod. (thousand tons)	**2,600**	**2,450**	**5**	**80**	**2,080**	**190**	**27.5**	**40**	**n.a.**
Current Acreage (thousand hectares)	1,300	350	25	200	65	190	25	40	n.a.
Current Yield (tons/ha)	2.0	7	0.2	0.4	32	1.0	1.1	1.0	n.a.
Potential Yield Low Case (tons/ha)	2.7	10	0.3	0.6	60	1.3	1.5	1.3	n.a.
Potential Yield High Case (tons/ha)	3.2	12	0.4	0.7	75	1.8	1.7	1.5	n.a.
Price (US$/ton)	140	55	7,000	1,000	20	160	700	400	n.a.
Current Value (US$ million)	**364**	**135**	**35**	**80**	**42**	**30**	**19**	**16**	**721**
Additional Value Low Case (US$ million)	**127**	**58**	**18**	**40**	**36**	**9**	**7**	**5**	**300**
Additional Value High Case (US$ million)	**218**	**96**	**35**	**60**	**56**	**24**	**11**	**8**	**508**

Note: Assumes market distortions (e.g., low prices and access to fertilizers) are removed.
Source: INSTAT and World Bank staff estimates.

2.31   At the product-specific level, rice production has failed to keep up with population growth rates and productivity has stagnated, resulting in a continued reliance on imported rice, despite the country's potential. Until the mid-1990s, the weak supply response was attributable to several factors. The high price of fertilizers for small farmers and the deterioration of the infrastructure are a major handicap to the modernization of the sector.

2.32   In this context, the State should move expeditiously to divest itself of the many agricultural and agro-business industries still publicly owned, and of its involvement in the sugar and cotton markets. Vigorous pursuit of reform is also justified by the large unrealized potential in the agricultural sector. Table 2.1, for example, argues that the direct value of the agricultural sector output could increase by US$300 to US$500 million in the next 10 years if Madagascar manages to return to yield levels that match its past performance, if it achieves the potential envisaged by sectoral experts, and if distortions to production and to the distribution markets of inputs and agricultural products are removed. This implies annual growth rates of between 3.5 and 5.5 percent. These numbers are purely speculative, and large investments are required to restore or create the necessary infrastructure. They serve, however, to suggest the country's potential if the policies that would foster this change are implemented. We must also point out that our assumptions are conservative.

2.33   There is also large potential in livestock. Since the reopening of the European Union market in 1989, meat exports have expanded rapidly, rising from 150 tons to 3,790 tons, or about US$8 million worth, by 1995. An even larger potential remains largely untapped. Madagascar could earn US$17 million by filling the European Union quota of 7,500 tons. Current dairy production could be increased under an ongoing World Bank project, the livestock sector program. This project addresses constraints on agriculture through (i) supporting the withdrawal of the public sector from production activities; (ii) providing research and extension services aimed at increasing productivity (e.g., 44,000 artificial inseminations were envisaged for 1996); (iii) assisting in the development of private animal health service centers; (iv) implementing eradication programs for animal diseases; and (v) developing instruments to provide rural credit.

2.34   The agricultural sector also needs reforms in the institutional sphere to complement the liberalization that began a decade ago (see Box 2.4). In addition to dismantling the government interventions described above, the major constraints that still limit the growth of the agricultural sector include lack of access to finance and constraints on the diffusion of technological information and other know-how.

2.35   The first of these constraints, lack of access to finance (mainly by small farmers), is closely related to the lack of financial institutions aimed at supporting these producers. A state-owned bank, BTM, purportedly finances agriculture activities, but only 5 percent of its loans are for the rural sector, and loans to agriculture are highly concentrated on a few products and these primarily go to large farmers. Where credit has been available for small farmers, these producers have raised output by purchasing inputs (particularly fertilizers), making improvements to their land and building storage facilities. Facilitating the flow of credit in rural operations through the diversification of financial institutions is key to Madagascar's economic development, and is largely dependent on the resolution of other issues. For example, as previously discussed, land-tenure issues need to be addressed, as land titles could be used by farmers as collateral for credit.

2.36   Another constraint to the development of the agricultural sector relates to the limited diffusion of modern technology and know-how to farmers. The government should emphasize the provision of public agricultural services, in particular research and extension services. Research has recently made significant progress, but the results have not been appropriately disseminated. Extension services remain weak as a result of limited technical capacity, logistical problems of distribution, lack of coordination efforts, and weak links with research. These operational services deficiencies can be addressed through a more decentralized support.

Box 2.4: Lessons from Agricultural Liberalization

Over the last decade, the government has deregulated most agricultural prices and progressively eliminated export taxes, the last being the export tax on vanilla, which was abolished in May 1997. Real exchange-rate adjustments culminated in a flexible exchange-rate policy in 1994. In the livestock sector, the government has adopted a legal and regulatory framework aimed at privatizing the veterinary health services and livestock multiplication centers still in public hands. However, the cotton and sugar sub-sectors are still subjected to restricted trade measures and remain under State control. The impact of reforms has, therefore, been mixed. Nevertheless, two trends are discernible, in areas where liberalization has occurred, and in those where much remains to be done.

Liberalized Sectors

• *Fisheries exports* expanded rapidly after 1983, and generate more foreign earnings than the traditional agricultural exports. Earnings in 1997 totaled US$57 million.

• *Rice production* has also responded positively to the reforms, and accounts for most of the recent growth in the crop sector. The gradual elimination of the cheap urban food policies that were initiated in the early 1990s has resulted in increased activity by private traders and processors, higher farm-gate prices for rice paddy, and the elimination of the large rice deficits of recent years. Imports of rice have been reduced, and liberalization of the market has benefited producers. Increases in rice production, however, have been limited by subsidy of rice imports.

• Structural adjustment policies also raised the profitability of local production of *milk, live cattle, maize,* and *fruits*. Domestic liberalization made transport between producing and consuming regions profitable, opened up regional markets, and brought in foreign investment and know-how. These products also benefited from the adoption of a flexible exchange rate. This experience demonstrates that the agricultural sector can swiftly respond to better incentives.

Less-Liberalized Sectors

The impact of the adjustment measures on traditional exports, mainly cotton and sugar, was disappointing in aggregate terms. The output volume for these products declined by about 56 and 64 percent respectively over the period 1989-97. This poor performance is explained in part by the significant drop in world prices for vanilla and cloves; public monopolies (HASYMA, for cotton, and SIRAMA and SIRANALA for sugar); and the continuing deterioration of the transport infrastructure that perpetuates private monopolies and low farm-gate price. Output of crops under public monopoly has been restrained by producer prices below world prices. Cotton production fell from 41,000 tons in 1989 to 26,000 tons in 1990. Sugar production has been too low to fill the US and EU quotas.

2.37   **Mining**. The mining sector is one of the candidates that would most obviously benefit from an improvement in the judicial system and a more modern regulatory framework, and has the potential for exports of mineral resources totaling US$500 million to US$600 million by the end of next decade, from about US$25 million in 1997. Foreign investment in big mining projects is the key to realizing this potential. Two pending large projects (QIT/RTZ, titanifer sands; and Phelps Dodge, nickel and cobalt) will enable exports of US$400 million a year after the required investment of about US$900 million has been made during the next 15 years. Production in both cases is scheduled to begin by the middle of the next decade. Other mineral products, such as semiprecious stones and gold, also have export potential. These products are currently being smuggled in large quantities, but if directed through official channels they could represent exports of close to US$100 million. For these estimates to become reality, however, the government must move from favoring small-scale mining activities dominated by Malagasy firms to a more open investment environment. It can model reforms on those of countries like Argentina, Chile, and Peru, which have successfully attracted investment into the sector.

2.38   Several areas of reform are necessary to develop the mining sector. The tax regime for the sector is too complex and must be simplified. To facilitate investment, the government could adopt model investment agreements to facilitate entry and to clarify the rules governing the sector. The agreements would eliminate all regulatory constraints on marketing and foreign exchange controls, and would concurrently establish an equitable taxation system. In addition, the 1995 Mining Code and its implementation decrees and regulations need to be updated to enshrine the above-proposed changes in law. Revisions should also provide for a clear allocation of jurisdiction over mining rights, non-discriminatory access to mineral rights, transparency and accountability of the mineral rights regime, security of tenure, and for a neutral dispute resolution system such as the International Center for the Settlement of Investment Disputes, or other arbitration mechanism for solving commercial disputes. Also, OMNIS (the *Office Militaire National des Industries Stratégiques*) would need to be transformed into a regulatory and geological information agency, without any activities in exploration, production, or commercialization; and KRAOMA (the *Société de Chromite de Madagascar*) should be privatized. It is also imperative to clear the backlog of concession applications within rules that favor the environmentally safe development of these mining areas.

2.39   **Tourism**. Madagascar measure 587,000 square kilometers and has a population of 14.2 million. The annual arrival of tourists increased in 1997 to 112,000, or 35 percent more than in 1996 and more than double the number that arrived in the early 1990s. This represents an annual growth rate during the 1990s of about 10 percent. In contrast, Mauritius, which measures 1,700 square kilometers and has a population of 1.2 million, receives more than 400,000 tourists a year.

2.40   Madagascar can aim at attracting tourists from South Africa, Reunion, France and other European countries, as well as tourists originating in East Asian countries who can combine Eastern or Southern African safaris with a visit to Madagascar (see Table 2.2 for more information). In particular, and unlike Mauritius and Seychelles, which specialize in beach tourism, Madagascar's diversity could allow it to adopt a tourism strategy that targets all market segments, from traditional holiday makers seeking a change of scenery to those in search of beaches, and to those interested in more adventurous and sophisticated activities such as eco-tourism.

2.41   Further development of the sector will not be easy. Concerted action is required in three areas: air access policy, visa requirements, and tourism infrastructure. Liberalization of air access policies is required to facilitate improvements in service and decreases in air transport prices. Unless air access policy firmly moves from protecting the interests of Air Madagascar, the growth in tourist numbers will be modest. Madagascar is a potentially interesting tourist destination, but the country remains a backwater with a small and uninteresting market for the airlines of the world. In contrast, Air Mauritius carries about two times the annual number of international passengers for all of Madagascar. The government should reconsider its policy of insisting on reciprocity of treatment for Air Madagascar (or any other Malagasy carrier), as this guarantees that airlines with a large load potential and a well-developed international network will not come to Madagascar.

Table 2.2: Madagascar, Unlocking Tourism Potential

MADAGASCAR

	1987	1990	1993	1996	1997
Tourism Revenues (US$ mill.)	6.0	29.9	27.8	44.6	67.0
Number of Tourists	28,136	52,923	55,355	82,681	112,200
Annual Growth Rates	87-97	90-97	93-97	96-97	
in Tourism Revenues	25.4	9.8	19.9	50.2	
in Number of Tourists	14.8	11.3	19.3	35.7	

OTHER COUNTRIES

	Tourism Foreign Exchange Earnings (US$ millions)				Annual Growth Rates		
	1980	1985	1990	1993	80-93	85-93	90-93
Barbados	252	311	500	528	5.9	6.8	1.8
Jamaica	241	407	740	943	11.1	11.1	8.4
Philippines	320	506	466	1178	10.5	11.1	36.2
Kenya	239	249	465	422	4.5	6.8	-3.2
Mauritius	42	56	244	304	16.4	23.5	7.6
Morocco	453	606	1280	1234	8.0	9.3	-1.2
Tunisia	684	558	1020	1225	4.6	10.3	6.3

Source: Staff estimates and Ministry of Tourism.

2.42   Much has been done during 1997 to facilitate the granting of tourist visas, a process that can now be carried out at the airports. In addition, exit visas have been abolished. A recent survey carried out in Madagascar suggests that the current system of visas has worked satisfactorily in facilitating tourism; the country could, however, adopt a more open visa policy similar to those of other countries in the region, combating risks such as drug trafficking with other mechanisms of control. Increased emphasis on information technology at the main points of entrance is likely to increase tourist satisfaction and help facilitate security control, for example.

2.43   Madagascar will soon face supply-side constraints due to the poor condition of its infrastructure and the limited number of lodging facilities. However, if a strategy that facilitates the development of hotels in key areas is pursued, including solving the land tenure issues that make hotel construction more difficult, the country could receive foreign exchange earnings from the tourism sector equivalent to about US$200 million after 10 years. This would also require improving the road and water supply infrastructure of key areas such as Diego Suarez, Fort Dauphin, and Nosy Be.

CHAPTER 3

ADAPTING THE STATE TO A NEW ROLE

STRATEGY FOR PUBLIC SECTOR REFORM

3.1   Madagascar needs to develop a modern State capable of playing an important role in reducing poverty and alleviating its effects. The challenge for the country and its policy makers is to design a public sector reform strategy that achieves this goal while concurrently supporting economic development. Success in implementing such a strategy requires careful sequencing of reforms. For example, there is widespread agreement that public expenditures in basic health care services and primary education are too low. Simply increasing these expenditures within the current state of government organization would be, however, a recipe for waste and failure. In addition, increased government revenues would enable an increase in expenditures while maintaining a fiscal deficit consistent with a sustainable macro framework, but how these revenues are increased is at least equally relevant.

3.2   This chapter aims to offer some reflections on how to build a reform strategy for the public sector. We first examine the revenue side of public finances, and stress that government revenue policy should not only aim at increasing public savings, but also at encouraging private savings and economic efficiency. In this regard, action is required to improve tax collection, mainly through broadening the tax base and combating tax fraud. Non-tax revenues can also contribute an important share of the increase in revenues, particularly through collecting fees for economic activities where the government's revenue should reflect more closely the value of the natural resource (e.g., fishing and mining license fees). With appropriate policies, revenues should increase from the current level of about 9.5 percent of GDP (see Table 3.1), which is a level comparable to that of countries suffering from civil disorders and war.

3.3   Acting on the expenditure side is also of utmost importance, and is the subject of the following section. Public spending on education, health, and essential infrastructure is below that of other Sub-Saharan African countries. Increased expenditure will also require generous and well-managed donor support. Based on international experience, non-interest current expenditures can be expected to increase from about 7.6 percent of GDP in 1997 to about 11 percent by the year 2008. Capital expenditures could increase slightly, from about 7 percent of GDP to more than 8 percent. It is not only more spending that is necessary to address the developmental bottlenecks for which the State is responsible, however; this section also proposes ways to make that government spending more effective.

3.4   Institutional and organizational structural changes must be introduced. For example, primary school teachers and health nurses and administrative agents could be redeployed from around the region of Antananarivo, where there is excess staff, to inadequately covered rural areas, thereby enabling an improved delivery of essential services to the poor. This transfer of human resources, together with the introduction of reforms to develop a more effective civil service, is required for better control and management of revenues and expenditures, and a closer link between demand and supply of government-provided goods and services. These structural changes will also translate into shifts in resources. For example, the wage bill is expected to increase from 3.3 percent of GDP in 1997 to 4.4 by 2003, and a well-designed decentralization policy will imply additional resources being transferred to local governments.

Table 3.1: Madagascar, Fiscal Developments for the Next Two Decades, High-Growth Scenario

	1997	2000	2005	2010	2015
Real GDP Growth	3.6	4.8	7.0	7.5	7.5
Percentage of GDP					
Total Government Revenues	9.7	12.2	15.5	17.1	17.1
Total Government Expenditures	17.4	18.7	19.7	20.0	19.9
Current Expenditures	10.9	10.9	11.7	11.7	11.6
Wages and Salaries	3.4	4.0	4.5	4.5	4.4
Goods and Services	2.5	2.4	2.8	3.0	3.2
Interest Expenditures	3.0	1.8	1.3	0.8	0.5
Transfers	2.0	2.7	3.1	3.4	3.5
Capital Expenditures	6.5	7.8	8.1	8.3	8.3
Fiscal Deficit (before grants)	-7.7	-6.4	-4.2	-3.0	-2.8
Fiscal Deficit (after grants)	-2.4	-2.1	-1.3	-1.1	-1.6

Note: Transfers to local governments are expected to increase while transfers to national public entities are assumed to steadily decline.
Source: Ministry of Finance and staff estimates.

3.5   In sum, concerted action is required not only on the revenue and expenditure side of public finances, but also on the institutional and organizational fronts. While the sequence of reforms is important, achieving results is subject to considerable uncertainty. For example, reform in the area of decentralization may not be an easy endeavor given the current weaknesses at the level of the central government administration. In fact, there is no guarantee that increasing transfers to local governments will not encounter similar deficiencies. Also, increasing revenues by broadening the tax base requires examining many of the existing tax regimes and exemption mechanisms, such as the special regimes authorized by the export processing *zone franche* and the 1989 investment code. This requires decisive government action, and performance can be expected to be uneven. It is important to act on the areas recommended in this chapter, but also to maintain a consistent macroeconomic framework. To avoid resource waste, increases in expenditures should be tied to improvements in their effectiveness in alleviating poverty and in supporting economic growth. Closely monitoring developments in the public sector reform agenda will enable the identification of additional needs and adoption of corrective policies.

REVENUES: EFFICIENCY AND EQUITY

3.6   Tax collection fell from a peak of 14 percent of GDP in 1987 to a low of 7.8 percent in 1994 (see Table 3.2). With the resumption of economic growth, the tax ratio recovered to about

9 percent of GDP in 1997. To finance a modern state supportive of growth, however, tax collection over the next decade will need to increase further: a target of 15 percent of GDP — the current average for Sub-Saharan Africa — seems reasonable. A greater role could also be played by non-tax revenues, given the many renewable and non-renewable natural resources from which the State could aim to increase its revenue share. Total revenues could rise to 17 percent of GDP in about 10 years, from the current level of about 9.5 percent.

3.7   What are the main reforms that need to be introduced on the revenue side? Action is required to strengthen the fiscal and custom administration to increase the base on which government revenues are levied, with special attention being given to tax efficiency issues. Also, tax equity issues should be examined, particularly taxes on hydrocarbons. Improving collection does not require extensive tax legislation reform, as the system in place is broadly adequate and modern. What is required is a more critical evaluation of what has worked and what has not, and the introduction of modifications whenever necessary.

Table 3.2: Madagascar, Tax Performance, 1984-97

	Avg. 1984-88	1987	1988	1990	1992	Avg. 1989-92	1993	1994	1995	1996	1997	Avg. 1993-97
Percentage of GDP												
Total Taxes	**10.1**	10.9	10.5	9.4	8.7	**8.4**	8.2	7.7	8.3	8.5	9.1	**8.4**
Direct Taxes	**1.9**	1.8	1.7	1.6	1.4	**1.4**	1.7	1.8	1.4	1.7	1.9	**1.7**
Indirect Taxes	**8.2**	9.2	8.8	7.8	7.2	**7.0**	6.4	5.9	7.0	6.8	7.2	**6.7**
Domestic 1/	**4.4**	4.8	4.6	4.0	4.0	**3.7**	3.4	3.8	4.4	3.7	4.3	**3.9**
Imports 2/	**2.4**	2.5	3.0	3.0	2.8	**2.5**	2.8	1.9	2.3	2.9	2.9	**2.6**
Exports	**1.4**	1.9	1.3	0.8	0.5	**0.8**	0.2	0.2	0.3	0.1	0.0	**0.2**
Import Taxes as Percentage of Good Imports	**19.6**	20.4	22.3	16.2	17.8	**16.2**	18.7	10.5	11.5	18.1	15.7	**14.9**
Percentage of Total Tax Revenues												
Direct Taxes	**19.1**	16.0	15.8	17.3	16.5	**17.2**	21.2	23.1	16.2	20.1	20.6	**20.2**
Indirect Taxes	**80.9**	84.0	84.2	82.7	83.5	**82.8**	78.8	76.9	83.8	79.9	79.4	**79.8**
Domestic 1/	**43.7**	43.5	43.6	42.6	46.1	**43.6**	41.5	49.5	52.3	44.1	47.0	**46.9**
Imports 2/	**23.5**	22.7	28.5	31.6	31.9	**29.8**	34.6	25.2	27.6	34.4	32.0	**30.8**
Exports	**13.7**	17.7	12.1	8.5	5.5	**9.5**	2.6	2.2	3.9	1.4	0.4	**2.1**

Notes: 1/ includes VAT on imports, and 2/ excludes VAT on imports.
Source: Ministry of Finance and staff estimates.

3.8   **Fiscal and Custom Administration.** Taxpayers with similar incomes and consumption patterns often pay in Madagascar very different amounts of taxes. To some extent this is due to the lack of an effective control system within the government administration in charge of revenue collection, and to the unbalanced enforcement of tax legislation. Fiscal and custom administration authorities lack human and material means, and the situation is worsened by the splitting of the former *Direction des Impôts* into three branches, each with its own provisions for tax administration.

3.9   The focus of reform should be to improve collection by strengthening the capacity of the fiscal and custom administrations, introducing more transparency into assessments and creating a simpler and more easily administered tax-reporting system. Although slower than expected, the effort to improve the tax administration has gotten off to a good start, particularly with the creation in April 1997 of a large taxpayer unit, the *Centre Fiscal Pilote des Entreprises*, or CFPE. All firms with an annual turnover of at least FMG 250 million are subject to examination by the CFPE. For these firms, tax payments are now based on self-assessment and declaration and payment by the firm. Early results are encouraging, but the material means of the system, including computerization, need to be strengthened. In addition, there is a proposal to create a synthetic tax that would help small Malagasy enterprises (i.e., those with an annual turnover of less than FMG 250 million) meet their fiscal responsibilities. This tax would have a single and low rate, making it easier to enforce.

3.10   Collection of customs duties is far below potential, due mostly to tax fraud, abusive use of exemptions authorized under the export processing zone, and ad hoc tariff exemptions issued to favored entrepreneurs by government officials. This poor revenue performance occurs despite the fact that Madagascar has had for many years a contract with a well-known international firm specializing in customs securitization. These firms charge fees equivalent to 1 percent of the f.o.b. value of imports in order to monitor volumes and unit prices at the merchandise's port of origin. The main reason why this contract has been ineffective resides in its continuous modification. At times, the contract has excluded control for imports originating with many of the country's key trading partners, and contract clauses have precluded the company from controlling in cases where the actual payments made by the importer to the customs administration match the amount that had originally been assessed. Some of these deficiencies seem to have been addressed in a new contract signed between the company and the government and dated January 1998, but the effectiveness of the new contract will need to be monitored in the coming months.

3.11   Several additional measures are required to strengthen the fiscal and customs administration. Training programs and better information as to the responsibilities of taxpayers must be emphasized. It is necessary to strengthen the administration of all indirect taxes, but direct taxes will also need to be reevaluated. In this regard, tax rates, scales, and provisions for depreciation will need to be re-examined, and the CFPE needs to be strengthened further with the constitution of a single file for each taxpayer, including the use of identification numbers, and the revision of the incentive system for fiscal and customs administration staff.

3.12   **Tax Efficiency**. Because of its impact on relative prices and returns on investment, the taxation system, including fiscal incentive regimes, is a cornerstone of the private sector business environment. Unfortunately, the high level of exemptions is negatively affecting revenue collection, potentially compromising the sustainability of the macroeconomic framework and distorting market competition in many economic sectors. This disparity between potential and actual collection results in custom revenues on imports that amount to 16 percent of the import bill — this in a country with a weighted import tariff of more than 20 percent. Exemptions are continuously granted to public and private enterprises or institutions, denoting a discretionary decision-making process in the administration of public finances.

3.13   To address these deficiencies, it is imperative to adopt effective operational measures to closely monitor the exemptions stipulated in the Investment Code of 1989, and to evaluate Madagascar's export processing zone (EPZ). The Investment Code, which was eliminated in 1996, provides prejudicial tax advantages that have not been monitored, and as a result, abuse is widespread. Creation of employment and actual investments should be evaluated and, when appropriate, the special tax-exemption agreements envisioned in the Code should be canceled. Currently, it is estimated that 1 percent of GDP in government revenues is lost through these exemptions.

3.14   The fiscal administration must also verify the special tax regimes in force under the EPZ legislation. The status of EPZ firms must be reviewed, as it is estimated that additional revenues in an amount close to 1 percent of GDP are being lost through tax breaks offered to firms that are not exporting. For example, of the 167 firms with EPZ status in 1996, 66 had yet to export as of late 1997, even though imports had already taken place. Even those firms that have exported have imported goods for a larger amount, clearly suggesting that abuses are taking place as the law authorizes selling in the domestic market only 5 percent of total production. Also, in contrast to the EPZs in other countries, it is important to highlight that in Madagascar these enterprises are not located in any special zone but across the country, making their control a true and costly fiscal dilemma. In addition, VAT and tariff exemptions were offered to non-governmental organizations, and even private firms, on an ad hoc basis during 1996 and 1997. This preferential tax treatment is not justified, and in the case of many NGOs, the size of these institutions is too small to merit special exemptions. VAT also needs to be extended to a larger share of products, and an effective system of reimbursement to exporters must be introduced. As VAT collection improves, a reduction the tax rate from 20 percent to, say, 15 percent should be considered.

3.15   **Tax Equity**. After more than a decade of tax reform, tax legislation is broadly satisfactory on equity grounds. The tax system is progressive, with taxes on automobiles the most progressive, followed by taxes on gasoline. The only regressive tax (i.e., the poor pay in relative terms a larger share of the tax than the rich) is the tax on paraffin oil, which is used as a source of lighting and cooking by 80 percent of the population.

3.16   The main change required to increase equity would be to reduce the tax on paraffin oil. Raising the tax on gasoline can compensate for the impact on government revenues, and could in fact raise additional revenues. The scope for raising taxes on petroleum is large, since Madagascar has one of the lowest gasoline prices in the world — a price per liter of US$0.46 compared to US$0.78 in Albania, US$0.80 in Tanzania, US$0.66 in Malawi, US$0.67 in Nicaragua, and US$0.59 in India. The petroleum tax currently raises about 1 percent of GDP. Given the relatively low price of petrol, revenues could increase by 0.5 percent of GDP. Taxes on alcohol and tobacco could also be raised, but would not yield much revenue due to their small base.

3.17 **Non-Tax Revenues**. The most important (potential) non-tax revenue is that levied on the exploitation of natural resources. The final goal is not only to maximize government revenues, but also to do so within a framework that results in an environmentally sustainable exploitation of the natural resource. One of these revenue sources is the license fee on shrimp fishing. Currently, government revenues from the issuance of shrimp fishing licenses amount to US$700,000, or about 1 percent of the total value of shrimp production, which was estimated at about US$60 to US$70 million in 1997. This compares unfavorably with the fiscal revenues from shrimp fishing in other countries, which range from 5 to 10 percent of the total value of the resource. It is also consistent with other evidence that suggests that there are serious transparency issues involved in the allocation of these licenses. Similar potential revenue sources exist in the domain of mining licenses, revenues from chance games, such as lotteries, and forestry licenses.

EXPENDITURES: BETTER SERVICES FROM PUBLIC MONEY

3.18 The Malagasy public sector is currently unable to provide the level or quality of public goods and services required to achieve and sustain rapid economic growth. Investment in human capital and infrastructure are extremely inadequate, with the levels of spending in some areas among the lowest in the world. Faster revenue mobilization can be expected to lead to an increase in non-interest current spending of as much as 4 percentage points of GDP over the next 10 years. But public sector effectiveness in delivering public goods and services is low, and increases in available resources may not necessarily translate into improvements. In addition, the fiscal position is heavily dependent on foreign grants, with fiscal deficits of -7.7 and -2.4 percent of GDP — before and after grants, respectively — in 1997. This contrasts with the Sub-Saharan African averages of -5.5 and -2 percent, and suggests that Madagascar needs to gradually strengthen its fiscal accounts.

3.19 In this context, a two-fold strategy should be followed. In the first stage, emphasis must be on improving government resource allocation to produce a higher return on public spending, and on improving the non-grant balance position of public finances. The second stage will aim at a gradual expansion of primary education, basic health services, and infrastructure expenditures, among others. These increases should follow introduction of the many institutional and organizational changes discussed in the next section, particularly the decentralization of government expenditures.

3.20 An important aspect of the two-fold strategy described above is that the government enforce budgetary discipline, as better programming of expenditures will fail to improve the availability of public goods and services unless governance improves. As one example, the total social sector current expenditures in 1996 were programmed at FMG 374 billion (37 percent of total current expenditure), but only FMG 204 billion was spent (21 percent). If the leadership fails to respect budgetary rules and discipline, it is difficult to use the budget to regulate expenditures vis-à-vis both revenue performance and debt service constraints (see Box 3.1).

3.21 Provided the government maintains its commitment to an adjustment program and mobilizes donor support, expenditure per capita is set to gradually recover according to the high-growth scenario described in the first chapter (see Table 3.3). More specifically, total non-interest expenditure should gradually recover from a low of US$36 per capita in 1995 to US$45 by the year 2000, US$60 by 2005, and US$97 by 2015 (all in 1997 dollars). Public investment per person would have returned to its 1990 level, that is about US$26 per capita, by the middle of next decade. In turn, budget balance would strengthen, with fiscal deficits stabilizing before and after grants at about -2.4 and -1.3 percent of GDP. While non-interest expenditure per capita will increase to US$100 (in 1997 dollars) by 2015, Madagascar would still remain among the countries with the lowest expenditure level due to its low income.

Table 3.3: Madagascar, Non-Interest Expenditure per Capita in 1997 US$, 1985-2015

	1985	1990	1997	2000	2005	2010	2015
Capital Expenditures	15	22	18	21	26	33	42
Non-Interest Current Expenditures	29	23	19	24	33	43	54
Total Non-Interest Expenditures	44	45	37	45	59	76	96
of which: Education Expenditures	n.a.	7.2	5.3	6.2	8.2	10.5	13.3
of which: Health Expenditures	n.a.	3.4	3.4	4.0	5.3	6.8	8.6
Total Non-Interest Exp. as Share of GDP per Capita	14	15	15	17	18	19	19

Sources: Ministry of Finance and staff estimates. Excludes transfers to universities.

3.22 Government can affect distribution of welfare and the position of the poor through the allocation of benefits flowing from public spending. But it is not only the need to help the poor that should trigger government expenditures — public goods and services should also aim at facilitating both economic and social development. For example, spending more (and more wisely) on education not only benefits the whole Malagasy population, but also makes the country more attractive to investors in search of a well-educated labor force. The following paragraphs discuss how expenditures in health, education, and infrastructure could be improved.

3.23 **Health**. Indicators of the health of the Malagasy population show somewhat worse results than those for other Sub-Saharan African countries. For example, access to safe water is limited to 32 percent of the population, well below the Sub-Saharan African average of 47 percent. Tuberculosis cases are 310 per 100,000 inhabitants, one of the highest rates in Africa. Child immunization complies with regional averages, at 59 percent for measles and 67 percent for DPT. Child malnutrition affects one-third of the population under the age of five, and is among the worst of the African countries.

3.24 The 1998 budget for health has been programmed at US$55 million, or about 1.5 percent of GDP, of which US$27 million is for current expenditures and US$28 million for capital expenditures. The distribution is excessively centralized, with 41 percent of total resources being spent at the central level, 9 percent at the regional level, and 50 percent at the district level. The health budget signifies expenditure of about US$4 per capita for Madagascar's population of about 14.5 million. With the current estimate of an additional US$4 per person of private expenditure, total expenditure per capita on health is about US$8. This is less than the recommended minimum for low-income countries of about US$10 per capita, implying that an important share of the population is inadequately covered.

Box 3.1: Recent Progress in Improving the Budget Process

The budget is both an instrument for the government to plan the allocation of scarce budget resources and a tool for control of the executive branch of government. Three areas of the budget process have seen remarkable improvements during the last few years. These are:

• **Budgetary Framework**: The Budget Law now reflects exhaustively the financial operations of the central government, and includes: (i) all revenues (cash basis) including transfers in the Central Bank (balance of payments aid); (ii) cash payments of external public debt service; and (iii) all public investment program grants and in-kind grants. This new budgetary framework is therefore coherent with the data managed by other government departments, and is consistent with the balance of payments.

• **Budget Implementation**: In order to accelerate budget implementation, the distribution statements (*états de répartition*) and the programs of utilization (*programmes de répartition*) have been suppressed. To complement this measure, the agreed-upon Budget Law is presented with an annexed document, known as the Execution Budget, which provides a more detailed description.

• **Budget Execution**: Budget execution should comply with three fundamental principles. These are simple procedures, decentralized execution, and effective monitoring of accounts. While much has been done to strengthen budget execution, it is still insufficient. For example, decentralization of budget management has to be effective at two levels: (i) the ministers must be in charge of the annual credits given to them for the relevant activities of their ministry, and (ii) the principal treasuries have to extend authority to allow regional execution of expenditures.

Notwithstanding the progress achieved, the budget process exercise is not yet working in a satisfactory manner for several reasons. Among them, extrabudgetary expenditures have become almost unchallenged, resulting in the accumulation of budgetary arrears for justified expenditure. Transfers to autonomous agencies and local governments are also not monitored.

What can be done to improve this performance? Now that the technical work to improve budget procedures is near completion, it is necessary for the Presidency and the Prime Minister to require enforcement from their Ministers. The Regional Treasury offices also need to be linked with the Central Treasury, enabling the consolidation of information on payments following budget line classification. Action in these areas would also reflect commitment to improved governance.

3.25   In terms of human resources, Madagascar is better equipped than most other African countries. The country has one medical doctor per 12,273 persons and one nurse per 4,090 persons, compared to Sub-Saharan Africa's 18,480 and 6,532, respectively. The public health staff is almost sufficient to meet World Health Organization recommended targets. Madagascar is also relatively well-equipped in terms of infrastructure, with 87 hospital and 1,812 basic health facilities. These centers cater for almost three-quarters of the poor and, if operating optimally, could treat more than 80 percent of the diseases that afflict the poor.

3.26   There is, therefore, a wedge between resources spent — where Madagascar lags — and physical and human resources of the health sector — where Madagascar ranks well. Why then such a dismal performance in health indicators? The answer is to a large extent linked to staff distribution, with an over-concentration in the urban areas, particularly Antananarivo. For example, the 21 percent of the population in urban districts is served by 41 percent of the staff. Similarly, in urban districts there are 2.3 doctors per 10,000 persons, while rural districts have 0.4 doctors. This is consistent with the fact that most secondary and tertiary care facilities are located in urban centers. These facilities also serve the rural population, but a better balance in staff distribution is possible. In addition, salaries are low and incentives are inadequate. Poor personnel policy results in a high turnover of health care staff, and a situation in which staff appointments are made on political grounds.

3.27   In the future, public spending is to be concentrated on prevention, with emphasis on acute conditions and especially communicable diseases, improved immunization coverage, enhanced access to essential drugs, increased emphasis on information campaigns for family planning methods, and strengthening management capacity within the sector. There is an urgent need to raise health budget expenditure in rural districts; to allocate budgets at the district level according to the number of primary health facilities; and to define modalities for cost recovery to allow all districts to secure additional resources as a basis for improving service quality. As these structural changes are introduced and take a firm hold, it will be possible to increase expenditure. It is also worth mentioning that there is extensive cost-recovery for drugs and services. Funds generated are used to replenish drug stocks and to offer financial incentives to health care providers. The increase in non-interest expenditures described before and the high growth rates discussed in Chapter 1 would enable public health expenditure to increase to about US$9 per capita (in 1997 dollars) by 2015.

3.28   **Education**. Madagascar is one of the very few developing countries in Africa that had reached near-universal primary education in the early 1980s. Moreover, higher education was valued and recognized by many neighboring countries. However, following more than a decade of poor economic and sectoral management, the gross enrollment ratio in primary education has fallen back to about 73 percent, and the quality of education and training has declined dramatically. According to the 1993 census, fewer than half of children of school age (i.e., six to 14 years old) were attending school, and the rate of illiteracy among the young is now higher than among young adults and adults under 50. The toll of these developments will extend well into the future, particularly because those individuals who do not have formal education will have serious difficulties integrating into economic life.

3.29   The government spends approximately 3 percent of GDP on education, compared to an average of nearly 4 percent in Sub-Saharan Africa. The 1998 budget on education was programmed at about US$103 million, or slightly less than 16 percent of the government budget, distributed two-thirds into current expenditures and one-third into capital expenditures.

The breakdown between levels is: (i) primary and secondary education, US$83 million; (ii) technical education, US$5 million; and (iii) higher education, US$15 million.

3.30   The distribution of total education benefits (excluding university level) is mildly pro-poor (progressive) in relative terms, and pro-rich (regressive) in absolute terms. For example, the bottom quintile (20 percent) of the population, whom we might consider to represent the very poor, account for 10 percent of all public school benefits and only 5 percent of total expenditures. However, even this modestly favorable result is the outcome of the large number of children in poor households. As Table 3.4 shows, the bottom quintile receives about 15 percent of primary school benefits, but only 2 percent of secondary-I (i.e., first phase of secondary education) benefits and practically nothing from secondary-II education (i.e., second phase). On the other hand, while the richest quintile receives approximately its own share of primary school benefits, it garners about one-half of benefits from secondary-I education and 72 percent of secondary-II education benefits. Put differently, the rich receive only 40 percent more benefits than the poor in primary education, but in excess of 700 times more in secondary-II education. In fact, the distribution has worsened so much that poorest 20 percent of the population receives only 8 percent of the total expenditures, compared to about 15 percent in Ghana, Kenya, and Malawi. In contrast, the richest 20 percent receives 40 percent of public education expenditures, compared to 21 percent in Ghana and Kenya, and 25 percent in Malawi.

Table 3.4: Distribution of Education Benefits (as a percentage of total education benefits)

	Poorest Quintile	Richest Quintile	Ratio Richest-Poorest
Primary	14.8	20.4	1.4
Secondary-I	1.8	49.6	27.5
Secondary-II	0.1	72.3	723

Source: Staff estimates.

3.31   The accounting explanation for these indicators is that enrollment as a percentage of eligible students decreases dramatically for the poor as one moves from primary toward secondary education. For example, while the enrollment rate among the children belonging to the poorest quintile is about 50 percent in the case of primary education, it is only 2 percent in the case of secondary-I education and less than 1 percent for secondary-II. In contrast, for the top quintile the enrollment rate goes from 100 percent at the primary level to 67 and 55 percent at secondary-I and secondary-II, respectively.

3.32   While the gross enrollment ratio in primary school is 83 percent for the population as a whole, there are large differences between groups. Urban areas are much better off than rural areas. The gross primary enrollment ratio in urban areas is 126 percent, while the equivalent figure in rural areas, where the majority of poor children live, is 73 percent. Gross secondary enrollment ratios are five times higher in urban areas (48 percent) than in rural areas (9 percent). Likewise, gross enrollment ratios at both the primary and secondary levels are much lower for the poor. At the primary level, the ratio is only 48 percent for the children of the poorest quintile, compared to 113 percent for the children of the richest quintile. At the secondary level, the contrast is even more acute, with a gross enrollment ratio of only 2 percent for the poorest quintile and 53 percent for the richest quintile.

3.33   The underlying factors that trigger these results are more worrisome. Low enrollment is the outcome of higher implicit costs borne by poor students and their families, as students in poor rural areas often have to walk further to school and, in particular, their help may be more needed at harvest times. There is also evidence of significant declines in attendance during the rainy season. The explanation given is that, once the rainy season begins, pupils find it more difficult to attend school. In sum, school attendance has a pronounced seasonal character: it is relatively high at the beginning of the school year, and then gradually declines. Often the students simply repeat the school grade the following school year, with the percentage of students who repeat classes approximating between 40 and 50 percent. Most of this is not due to exacting academic standards, but to the cessation of school attendance.

3.34   Under these conditions, it is important not only to redirect resources toward the poorer rural areas and to primary educational levels, but also to address the causes of low primary school enrollment rates among the poor. This requires providing more incentives for school attendance, such as tying school attendance to the provision of nutritional programs. The importance of highly educated labor — both in attracting foreign investment and in making domestic investment more productive — cannot be over-stressed. When enrollment rates increase at the primary level, it is likely that more students from poor families will continue their schooling to higher levels. The enrollment rates among the poor at higher educational levels may thus increase, and the balance of education benefits would shift more toward the poor than is currently the case. Improvements in primary education would also make it possible to design vocational training for the poor.

3.35   Finally, the government has recently adopted a series of policies and measures to address the issues in the education sector and to face the challenges of its transition to a global economy in the next century. The main elements are (i) a steep increase in public financing for high-quality, universal basic education; (ii) a small increase in public financing for secondary education, aimed at improving the efficiency of public schools and promoting a dynamic and aggressive role of private-sector and local communities; and (iii) the maintenance of public resources for higher education at their current level in the medium term. Autonomous universities and institutions of higher learning would be invited to finance a larger share of their own budget through the introduction of tuition fees and other cost-recovery and revenue-generation measures. As discussed in Table 3.3, it is expected that public expenditures per capita in education will increase from US$5 in 1997 to about US$13 by the year 2015 (in 1997 dollars).

3.36   **Infrastructure**. Lack of infrastructure in irrigation and roads restricts the expansion of agriculture as well as the efficiency with which land is used, thereby contributing to environmental degradation. Poor roads hamper the provision of inputs to export-oriented manufacturing enterprises and the agricultural sector. Infrastructure failures arise from (i) low budget allocations, particularly for maintenance of existing installations; (ii) inefficient administrative procedures concerning implementation; and (iii) inefficient public enterprises in critical areas like ports (particularly the port of Toamasina), railways, telecoms (TELMA), water and power (JIRAMA), airports (ADEMA), and river and coastal transport.

3.37   A multi-pronged approach is needed to address these problems. Privatization of remaining State companies, a subject discussed in Chapter 2, needs to be convincingly pursued within a regulatory framework designed to promote competition. In parallel, local communities must be empowered to maintain, rehabilitate, and eventually expand local infrastructure. Finally, efforts to attract private firms into the provision of infrastructure maintenance services need to be expanded. A good start has been made, with the *Agence d'Exécution des Travaux d'Interêt Public d'Antananarivo* (AGETIPA) undertaking urban works in Antananarivo. This example could be extended to other urban centers.

3.38   Improving the road network ranks high among Madagascar's development needs. The donor community has supported the earmarking of resources for road maintenance. The Road Maintenance Fund (*Fonds d'Entretien Routier*) was voted into law in October 1997 by the National Assembly, and is a first important step to facilitate road maintenance in Madagascar. In addition, it is necessary to define a regulatory framework and common-practice conditions for contracts, and to implement a network global programming framework based on clearly defined rehabilitation and maintenance strategies for feeder roads.

ORGANIZATIONAL AND INSTITUTIONAL CHANGES

3.39   The program of reallocation of public expenditures and of strengthening of revenue mobilization just discussed is wide-ranging, and will require concerted and determined action for a number of years. But an essential condition of this effort is a profound institutional modernization of the Malagasy government machinery. This will entail difficult changes on a number of fronts, among them the organization of the State and the capacity of its civil service. In short, the institutional reforms need to go beyond purely technical solutions and, perhaps above anything else, entail the need for the usually much more difficult change in culture. Experience shows that these changes take time, and for the most effective and lasting impact require the development of a profound dialogue within a country's civil society, together with imaginative and decisive leadership from the highest levels of government.

Civil Service and Public Sector Effectiveness

3.40   It will be difficult to implement the reforms recommended in this report with the current civil service organization. Despite the many laudable examples of devotion to public service, the civil service is unmotivated and unprepared to administer a reform program that favors private investment and reorients resources to the poor. There are several explanations for this environment, but the deterioration in public sector wages is among the most important. This has resulted in an increase in corruption as civil servants are increasingly forced to choose between integrity and survival, but it also benefits from the fact that the government excessively regulates economic activity.

3.41   To address these deficiencies, the government needs to (i) reduce the scope for corruption by simplifying procedures, eliminating whenever possible the need for official authorizations and licenses and decreasing the burden of government-imposed costs on private sector development; (ii) adopt a remuneration and employment policy for civil servants that provides the appropriate incentive framework; and (iii) strengthen the capacity to deliver goods and services, and thus support the alleviation of poverty and support economic growth.

3.42   The fight against corruption should take place on many fronts. In addition to adopting an effective remuneration and employment policy, it is necessary to eliminate discretionary decisions by public sector officials. To achieve this objective, the number of areas where government action is required should be reduced, and a clear and credible process for those individuals that wish to appeal government decisions should be introduced. Penalties for corruption must be high, and special emphasis should be given to showing that there has been a change in the tolerance of corruption cases by government authorities. The highest levels of government must be seen to be held to the same standards of conduct. Limiting the scope of action of the State through privatization and by liberalizing market competition would also help to eliminate opportunities for corruption.

3.43   Wages have declined in real terms by about 16 percent during the present decade, and by about 27 percent since the mid-1980s. The explanation for this deterioration lies with nominal wages not being able to keep up with inflation (see Table 3.5). In fact, the share of the wage bill in total government expenditures declined from about 34 percent in 1985 to 18 percent in 1994, only to recover to about 20 percent in 1997, indicating that the remuneration of civil servants was an important policy variable.

3.44   As revenue performance improves, there will be scope to correct the deterioration in civil service salaries. In 1997, the wage bill rose in real terms by 5 percent. It will continue to rise, reaching US$138 million in 1998, or 3.6 percent of GDP, up from 3.3 percent in 1997. This would represent about 20 percent of government expenditures. It will take some time to return to the 1985 level of US$150 million, however, and as a percentage of GDP is expected next decade to be at levels still well below the average of developing countries (4.5 percent compared to 6.7 percent in Africa, 4.9 in Latin America, and 4.7 percent in Asia).

3.45   What else needs to be done? Any dynamic society needs a modern and effective civil service. Madagascar is no exception. Appropriate incentives for civil servants must be introduced that extend beyond simple remuneration. In a first stage, the government has decided to give special emphasis to those units expected to jump-start the public administration in its revised role as a facilitator of private sector activity. As a result, senior technical and managerial staff of key ministries are expected to benefit from performance-based pay schemes, as practiced in Bolivia and other developing countries. To this end, the government has identified some 120 key policy and technical positions, and a strategy of wage-scale decompression has been announced by the government, though its implementation in 1997 and 1998 has been less than satisfactory.

3.46   Finally, to strengthen the implementation capacity and to facilitate the provision of public goods and services, the government could plan, within the framework of a civil service and institutional capacity building program, to reform the framework and management of public services and to strengthen institutions and actions to increase revenue. It should also plan to improve its audit and inspection procedures. In addition, the government contracting system must be strengthened by, for example, adopting a procurement code aimed at redefining the roles of the different participants involved, including reducing their number; and by radically simplifying the procedures and channels for signing contracts and making payments to contractors.

Table 3.5: Madagascar, Trends in Civil Service Personnel Expenditure, 1985-97

	1985	1990	1991	1992	1993	1994	1995	1996	1997
Nominal Civil Service Wage Bill Increases (%)	n.a.	n.a.	6.8	13.4	5.0	21.4	47.4	24.4	14.8
Real Civil Service Wage Bill Increases (%)	n.a.	n.a.	-6.2	0.8	-7.1	-14.2	1.5	5.4	4.6
Wage Bill/GDP (%)	5.3	4.0	4.0	4.0	3.6	3.1	3.1	3.2	3.3
Wage Bill/Government Expenditures (%)	32.2	23.7	24.4	20.7	18.2	16.8	17.7	18.1	21.5
Wage Bill (millions of 1997 US$)	151	122	106	119	121	92	98	128	116
Wage Bill per Person (US$)	1167	942	819	980	1009	779	834	1091	990
Number of Civil Servants (thousands)	129.0	129.7	129.7	121.1	120.3	118.1	121.3	120.5	135.5

Source: Ministry of Finance.

Deconcentration and Decentralization: Creating a State Responsive to People's Needs

3.47   Madagascar's history of unbalanced influence by the Antananarivo region over the rest of the country has produced a deeply felt need for administrative decentralization. This is also now enshrined in the Constitution, which allows for three levels of local government: municipal, regional, and provincial. Municipalities with elected mayors have been in place since late 1995, with responsibilities for local infrastructure and the provision of services. The performance of municipalities remains, however, weak, and most of the goods and services provided at this level of government are still largely being delivered through piecemeal donor interventions. The challenge is to address these deficiencies to make the most out of the resources spent at the municipality level (see Table 3.6).

3.48   The limited resources available to municipalities explain their weak performance. Out of the 1,428 communes created (1,392 in 1995 and 36 in 1997), ranging in size from a few hundred to nearly a million people, there are few with any significant resources or with truly qualified personnel. Local tax revenues are low, and are compounded by a tradition of non-payment of either fees or taxes and a reliance of local administrators on central government transfers. In addition, there are no incentives for municipalities to improve their performance, and for the past two years transfers to municipalities have been based on a system of block grants of FMG 30 million per municipality, for current expenditures, regardless of population size, and of FMG 302 million per *fivondronana* (i.e., district) for investment. A *Comité Local de Développement* has been created at the level of the district, as a public body empowered, on a transitory basis, to determine the use of resources allocated by the government as investment funds for the municipalities. Donors spend at least four times as much at the local level than the central government itself, but rarely use their funds to create incentives for communes to improve their management of infrastructure. Finally, the current institutional arrangements multiply the sources of conflict; between the mayor and the council, both elective bodies; and between municipal governments and deconcentrated central administration offices.

Table 3.6: Resources Spent at the Local Government Level, 1996

	FMG billion	US$ million	Percentage of GDP
Total Transfers	85	17.0	0.43%
o.w.: Lump-Sum Transfers a/	75	15.0	0.38%
Taxes Transferred b/	10	1.9	0.05%
Own Revenues	36	7.2	0.18%
Total	**121**	**24.2**	**0.61%**

Note: a/ This is the FMG 302 million per *fivondronana* (equivalent to the department), added to the FMG 30 million per municipality. b/ Taxes transferred or *ristournes*.
Source: World Bank staff estimates.

3.49   Extremely limited central government resources and the need to improve the overall tax to GDP ratio in a politically sustainable manner imply the need to revise the decentralization policy. This can be done around three key objectives: (i) minimize the administrative cost of decentralization; (ii) improve local-government performance in cost recovery and collection efficiency; and (iii) foster efficient use of limited central government and donor funds. Key elements of this strategy will be improved accountability and control mechanisms, as well as an important capacity-building program at the local level.

3.50   The institutional reform should focus on strengthening municipalities and eliminating sources of conflict, and also on limiting the costly multiplication of levels and institutions. For example, it has been proposed that the number of municipalities should be increased. This is a worrisome development given their already very small size — the average population of 1,498 municipalities is about 7,600. The responsibilities assigned by the decentralization laws to the provinces (construction and management of high schools, main hospitals, and provincial roads) and the regions (construction and management of junior high schools and secondary hospitals) are best left under the management of deconcentrated bodies of the corresponding ministries, and coordinated at the regional level.

3.51   The central government has also begun a process of rationalization of the administration to improve the workings of deconcentrated agencies of line ministries; to develop the ability of the *governor* or *préfet* to help them coordinate their actions; to enable the *sous-préfet* to provide ex-post legality control of municipal acts; and to ensure the role and structure of the territorial administration is supportive of, rather than in conflict with, local governments. While these are welcome developments, the government still needs a rational and comprehensive plan for deconcentration of line ministries. The current trend whereby ministries design their individual deconcentration plan is costly and results in unnecessary duplication.

Box 3.2: Block Grant System as an Incentive for Improved Tax Collection

Zimbabwe allocates block grants to municipalities, while closely monitoring their performance. Technical assistance teams are available at the regional level, but respond to the demand of local governments. At the end of an initial phase of two years, the local government is evaluated. The block grants of non-performers are turned into earmarked grants, while their responsibilities are decreased. Good performers are given more resources and responsibilities.

The main drawback of the system has been the cost of monitoring. It can also be difficult for municipalities to increase fees unless services are improved, which implies there may be a need to assist municipalities in upgrading some of their existing infrastructure. This could be done through an integration of donor financing within the overall government fiscal framework.

3.52   Reform of intergovernmental fiscal arrangements is also important, and should focus on improving collection efficiency and cost recovery in municipalities, strengthening local taxes as a revenue instrument, and ensuring that adequate resources are available to local governments. Concerning local taxes, the central government has proposed the suppression of the *octroi* (*taxe de roulage*). This will be compensated by greater powers given to municipalities concerning property tax — the main source of own revenues for urban municipalities — which will no longer be shared between different tiers of government. Block grants will now be allocated on the basis of population, and will be proportional to the amount of own resources collected. All municipalities, however, will be guaranteed a minimum amount. In addition, they will have access to a capital grant to fund local infrastructure projects on a first-come, first-served basis.

3.53   Examination of block grant spending in previous years shows that absorption capacity is extremely limited in rural areas, and that a major use of the grant has been "sitting" allowances for the municipal council. Further, there is no information available regarding the resource needs and potential of rural municipalities. The government, with donor assistance, has therefore embarked upon a program to help municipalities develop their absorption capacity, and to gather information on the expenditure needs of rural municipalities. It is hoped, however, that the government will introduce measures that would forbid the block grant to be used for financing of sitting allowances. Other systems can be considered, such as the system developed in Zimbabwe where transfers are linked to performance (see Box 3.2).

ECONOMIC DEVELOPMENTS DURING

TEN YEARS OF ADJUSTMENT

LESSONS FOR THE FUTURE

1988-1997

Overview

The economic recovery of the late 1980s was bluntly stopped in the early 1990s, first by a lengthy transition to democracy and then by political factionalism and policy differences on economic reform. As a result, the 1990s have been marked by declines in per capita income and increases in poverty. However, behind the overall poor performance, some ambitious policy decisions have been adopted. If implementation is not delayed, as was unfortunately the case during 1997, Madagascar has the potential of entering a period of sustained economic growth.

More specifically, after tentative adjustment in the early 1980s, by 1988 the country's leadership became convinced of the importance of an open economy. The exchange rate was adjusted to realistic levels, and an export-processing zone was set up to attract export-oriented investment. From 1988 to 1990, sustained per capita income growth was registered for the first time since 1972. Foreign investment rose from virtually nothing to US$22 million (close to 1 percent of GDP); private investment was set to overtake public investment, having risen from an average of 2.3 percent during 1983-87 to 8.5 percent by 1990; growth accelerated from an average of 1.4 percent over the period 1983-1987 to 3.5 percent from 1988-1990; and non-traditional exports almost doubled in value from 1986 to 1991, yielding US$233 million, representing 70 percent of total exports from about 30 percent in the mid-1980s. Over the same period, manufacturing exports almost tripled, to US$125 million. For the first time in many years, per capita GDP growth was positive, averaging more than half a percent annually over the years 1988-1990 (see Table A-1).

The process of economic liberalization contributed to political liberalization that resulted in a lengthy transition to democracy from 1991 to 1993. Political developments interrupted economic recovery and had a negative impact on economic activity, particularly in

1991 when GDP fell by 6.3 percent and large external payments arrears began to accumulate. Nevertheless, during the transition, investors and donors had high hopes that once the transition was completed, Madagascar would decisively opt for opening the country to foreign investment. These expectations were manifested by continued good performance of foreign investment. From 1991 to 1993, Madagascar received annually an average of US$17 million (0.6 percent of GDP) of foreign direct investment, close to the peak of US$22 million registered in 1990.

Table A-1: Madagascar, Selected Economic Indicators, 1983-1997

	Average 1985-87	Average 1988-90	1991	1992	1993	1994	1995	1996	1997
In percentages									
GDP Growth	1.4	3.5	-6.3	1.2	2.1	0.0	1.7	2.1	3.6
GDP Deflator	15.7	14.9	14.5	12.5	13.0	41.6	45.2	18.1	7.4
Poverty Head-Count Index	60	66	66	69	71	71	71	73	74
As percentage of GDP									
Trade Balance	-0.8	-3.4	-4.0	-4.7	-5.3	-3.3	-3.3	-3.0	-5.0
Current Account (before grants)	-9.0	-10.7	-12.3	-9.2	-9.9	-10.9	-10.2	-7.0	-7.8
Current Account (after grants)	-5.8	-5.5	-8.1	-5.0	-5.2	-7.0	-7.0	-3.7	-2.4
Tax Revenues	10.0	9.6	6.8	8.7	8.2	7.7	8.3	8.5	9.3
Non-Interest Expenditures	15.7	16.2	14.4	16.6	16.6	14.4	12.5	13.1	14.4
Fiscal Deficit (before grants)	-4.2	-5.8	-7.7	-10.1	-10.7	-11.5	-9.1	-9.1	-7.7
Fiscal Deficit (after grants)	-3.6	-2.7	-5.5	-6.8	-7.4	-8.5	-6.2	-4.9	-2.4
Investment	9.2	13.8	10.6	11.3	11.4	10.9	10.9	11.1	11.8
Private	3.1	5.7	4.6	3.1	3.7	4.7	5.2	5.0	5.5
Public	6.1	8.2	5.9	7.6	7.8	6.2	5.7	6.1	6.3
Gross Domestic Savings	4.1	7.7	0.7	3.4	2.5	3.4	3.6	5.8	4.7
In millions of US$									
Foreign Investment	0	12	14	21	15	6	10	10	14
In billions of US$									
External Debt	2.62	3.19	3.58	3.63	3.80	4.13	4.41	4.50	4.40

Source: INSTAT, IMF, and World Bank estimates.

A new democratic regime took office in 1993. Instead of moving forward with the reform agenda, economic recovery was blocked by political factionalism and policy differences on economic reform. The task of economic reform was also overwhelming in the existing political environment. Representatives of the established elite resisted attempts by more liberal policy-makers to open the economy. Despite strong advice from the donor community, a populist administration was initially seduced by the idea that development was possible without a significant opening to foreign investors. The government therefore pursued the illusory path of "isolationist economics," in an attempt to preserve economic independence and to implement an autonomous development strategy different from that adopted by successful developing countries. Although many of the economic policy decisions of the past were maintained, the reform program was slowed down and many temporary solutions adopted. In sum, the emerging consensus for reform remained fragile, and faced fierce action by the elite to defend the status quo — an economic strategy that had already proven its ineffectiveness.

In 1994, the first full year after the transition to democracy, the economic situation deteriorated and GDP stagnated, reflecting populist measures adopted by the incoming government in 1993. After the government allowed the exchange rate to float in May, resulting in a nominal devaluation of about 50 percent against the French franc, lax monetary management failed to prevent inflation rising to 61 percent by end-1994. In addition, structural imbalances were introduced through an increase in rice, flour, and petroleum subsidies, increasing the overall budget deficit after grants to 8.4 percent of GDP, the highest level since 1981.

In January 1995, the government replaced the deficient management of the Central Bank, agreed with the IMF on a stabilization plan to bring down the inflation rate, and declared its intention to implement adjustment policies. For 1995 as a whole, real GDP increased modestly by 1.7 percent (population growth was 3 percent); foreign investment increased to US$10 million; the budget deficit after grants was reduced to 6.1 percent of GDP; monetary conditions were tightened; the rate of inflation was lowered to 37 percent (at end-1995) — though still in excess of the 15 percent IMF target; and the real exchange rate depreciated, in a free market, by about 12 percent. However, an additional US$374 million of external payments arrears accumulated.

Meanwhile, tensions between the President and the Prime Minister (PM) slowed down decision-making on the reform front and led to a national referendum in September 1995. This referendum shifted authority to choose the PM from the National Assembly to the President. As a result, Mr. Rakotovahiny was named as PM by the President, and formed a government in November 1995. However, policy differences persisted as senior officials, led by the Minister of Finance, proposed to reverse key reforms. Steps were taken toward reactivating controls on private-sector activity, including prices, margins, and inventories; renewed government intervention in the import and marketing of rice was proposed; regulation of foreigners and issuance of visas were tightened; and liberalization of air transport and expansion of tourist facilities were stalled. In addition, the 1996 budget included public expenditures of questionable value at the expense of already underfunded social-sector expenditures. On the revenue side, a shortfall was expected because the government provided tax relief without adopting compensatory measures, including strengthened tax administration. Other key reforms, however, including rational pricing policies in energy, were maintained.

In May 1996, the President was urged to appoint a coherent economic team. At the same time, more than two-thirds of the parliamentary deputies supported a no-confidence vote against Mr. Rakotovahiny. This opened the way to the appointment of a non-political Prime Minister, Mr. Ratsirahonana, the former head of the Constitutional Court. The new PM wanted a government of openness to all political parties and of renewal, but he was not able to exclude a number of former ministers from previous governments. This set the stage for the National Assembly to impeach the President in August 1996. Mr. Ratsirahonana was appointed Acting Head of State, pending fresh Presidential elections, and appointed a broad-based government that moved decisively to adopt a comprehensive reform program. Reforms benefited from the support of all the key candidates during the election campaign, including former presidents Ratsiraka and Zafy. Both of them repudiated their earlier attempts at interventionist economic development strategies, and pledged to seek foreign-investment-led growth.

Economic performance initially remained weak due to the underlying political uncertainty. Foreign investment continued to recover, however, to US$10 million in 1996. Growth continued at the 1995 level of 2 percent. Inflation was brought under control and declined to 8 percent by year-end. The budget deficit after grants was further reduced to 4.9 percent (the lowest level since 1990), despite the continued poor performance of tax revenues. But the underpinnings for growth had been initiated. The reforms were supported by an ESAF approved by the IMF in November 1996 and a one-tranche World Bank Structural Adjustment Credit, approved in March 1997. Announcements on bank and enterprise privatization suggested the adoption of a more liberal and consistent economic policy stance. Sustainable fiscal and monetary policy, and improved developments in the external sector, set the ground for growth of about 3.6 percent in 1997. Inflation adopted a further declining trend, finishing 1997 with an end-of-year rate of 4.8 percent (CPI prices). However, as 1997 progressed, uncertainties increased as implementation of structural reforms lagged. This is particularly true in the area of privatization.

Much has happened in Madagascar since 1990. The balance of events is uncertain. While the country has changed, developments have been more disappointing than originally expected. There is widespread agreement within the international community that Madagascar's performance could have been better if the leadership had been seriously committed to reform. The next few pages attempt to provide a more thorough account of economic developments.

Real Sector

GDP growth has not kept up with population growth rates, resulting in a further decline in consumption per capita from US$251 in 1990 to US$227 in 1997. As a result, poverty increased from affecting 68 to affecting about 75 percent of the population. The poor performance since 1990 continues a trend that began in 1970, when per capita consumption reached US$473 (in 1997 prices).

As to sectoral performance, the agricultural sector has seen modest growth, averaging 1.9 percent annually since 1990. Rice, the most important of Madagascar's crops, has averaged an annual production increase of 0.5 percent, similar to that of other staple foods, with the exception of maize (see Table A-2). Maize output rose by 2.5 percent on average, almost keeping up with the population growth of 3 percent. Part of the difference in response between maize and rice can be attributed to the market of the former being free, while government continued intervention in rice until 1996. Perturbations in the rice market were also caused by imports that have been highly variable, and sold at prices not always reflecting market conditions. Export performance has been good, despite declines in the world market prices of the traditional exports: coffee, vanilla, cloves, and pepper (see Table A-3). With the exception of coffee, volumes have risen. More importantly, other agricultural exports have responded strongly to the liberalization measures adopted in the mid-1980s, rising from US$51 million (15 percent of total exports) in 1984 to US$112 million (23 percent of total exports) in 1996.

Table A-2: Madagascar, Agricultural Production 1990-96
(thousands of tons)

	1990	1991	1992	1993	1994	1995	1996
Rice Paddy	2,420	2,342	2,450	2,550	2,357	2,450	2,500
Manioc	2,292	2,307	2,280	2,350	2,360	2,400	2,353
Maize	155	145	130	165	155	177	180
Sweet Potato	494	488	450	500	560	450	500
Potato	274	273	275	280	270	275	280
Coffee	85	84	80	78	70	68	68
Vanilla	5	5	4	5	4	4	4
Cloves	14	15	12	17	14	13	13
Sisal	20	15	10	18	17	16	17
Cotton	32	27	20	25	27	24	26
Sugar Cane	2,000	1,950	1,900	1,950	2,166	2,100	2,150
Peanuts	30	30	23	32	28	30	36

Source: INSTAT.

Table A-3: Madagascar, Performance of Main Exports, 1990-1996

	Price Change 91-96 relative to 86-90	Volume change 91-96 relative to 86-90	Percentage of total exports in 1984	Percentage of total exports in 1996	Value of exports in mill. of US$ '84	'96
Coffee	-13%	-10%	42	14	141	68
Vanilla	-14%	n.a.	16	8	53	41
Cloves	-73%	51%	11	2	37	11
Pepper	-40%	7%	1	1	4	4
Traditional Exports (Coffee, vanilla, cloves, and pepper)	n.a.	n.a.	70	25	234	124
Other Agricultural Exports (shellfish, sugar, etc.)	n.a.	n.a.	15	23	51	112
Manufactured Exports	n.a.	n.a.	12	49	42	239
TOTAL	n.a.	n.a.	100	100	337	577

Source: INSTAT and World Bank estimates.

Mining has performed well below potential, with its formal contribution to GDP virtually stagnant since 1990 and remaining marginal. It added only US$10 million of value in 1996 (0.3 percent of GDP), and accounting for only 3.5 percent of total exports. Madagascar is best known for the production of chromite, graphite, and mica, but there have been a wide variety of other minerals produced in the country, including gold, quartz, and ornamental and semiprecious stones. Recent developments have focused on gold and gemstones, but they have taken place in the informal sector and production has been smuggled out of the country. Many other minerals have been identified (including titanifer sands, nickel, and cobalt), but foreign investments failed to materialize because of continued State intervention in the sector, cumbersome regulations, a lack of definition in the role played by key public institutions, and an overall disincentive to the development of mining operations on an industrial scale.

Table A-4: Madagascar, Selected Indicators of Performance in the Manufacturing Sector

	1990	1991	1992	1993	1994	1995	1996	1997
Value Added (in millions of US$)	336	294	318	359	323	342	428	364
Value Added (annual growth)	-1.8	-3.3	-3.5	1.6	4.1	0.1	1.2	0.9
Exports (millions of US$)	146	159	180	183	237	335	348	366
Exports (annual growth)	33%	9%	13%	1.5%	30%	41%	4.1%	5.1%
Openness (Exports plus Imports as percentage GDP)	32	32	30	28	39	42	33	33
Real Effective Exchange Rate (annual appreciation)	5.7	-12.7	6.4	10.6	-12.2	-9.3	24.7	-7.4

Source: INSTAT and World Bank estimates.

The private sector has shown serious interest in Madagascar's mining potential. A new graphite mine is currently under construction, with financing provided by South African investors. A US$400 million titanifer sands project sponsored by QIT/RTZ, one of the biggest mining corporations in the world, has been under negotiation for several years. More recently, Phelps Dodge, the biggest US copper producer, has shown interest in investing up to US$500 million in the development of a nickel-cobalt mine. Foreign investors complain however about the lack of attractiveness of mining's regulatory framework. There is too much State intervention in the sector, as seen by direct participation in mining projects, State control over the most promising mining rights, and excessive regulation of the commercialization and transportation of minerals. This has made negotiations with mining companies very difficult, and has proven a major disincentive for private investment in the sector.

Export diversification is also evident in the positive evolution of manufactured exports, which have risen from US$146 million (42 percent of total exports) in 1990 to US$348 million (63 percent) in 1996, and US$366 in 1997. This performance largely reflects the positive impact of the export-processing zone (EPZ) enterprises and the beneficial effects of a market-determined exchange rate. In 1994, a total of 66 EPZ enterprises accounted for 12 percent of formal-sector employment, 7 percent of manufactured output, 5.5 percent of sector value-added, and 24 percent of manufacturing exports. Moreover, manufacturing enterprises that export some of their output account for 52 percent of production, 55 percent of value-added, and 49 percent of employment in the formal-manufacturing sector. Their productivity is almost 10 percent higher than firms that do not export. While data on firm performance is not available for other years, the improved performance of the manufacturing sector, following the floating of the exchange rate in May 1994, is evident in the macroeconomic data (see Table A-4). Similarly, in 1996, as the exchange rate appreciated significantly, performance deteriorated.

The service sector continues to be the largest source of value-added (55 percent of GDP) and the growth of the sector has closely mirrored that of GDP. Services are dominated by community services (16 percent of GDP); transport (14 percent); trade (11 percent); and public administration (6 percent). Tourism-related earnings have grown unevenly from US$30 million in 1990 to US$45 million in 1996. In 1997, the sector observed a marked expansion, and the number of foreign tourists visiting Madagascar increased by 35 percent. Foreign exchange earnings rose to US$58 million.

Employment and Wages

The majority of the labor force is engaged in subsistence agriculture and informal-sector activities. Out of an economically active population of 5.6 million in 1995, an estimated 1 million have salaried employment. The vast majority of the remainder are in agriculture, although precise numbers are not available. Formal-sector employment is limited to 375,000, with about 150,000 in manufacturing, 125,000 in the civil service (with security forces), 80,000 in paid agricultural employment, and the remainder in the rest of the services sector.

The labor market has stagnated in terms of creation of formal wage employment, particularly with a virtual freeze on net public sector employment creation. Most entrants to the labor market have been absorbed by the informal sector. Unemployment is less than 3 percent of the labor force, with those who declare themselves unemployed estimated to number 115,000. Underemployment is widespread and affects 85 percent of the labor force.

For the private sector, the decline in wages largely reflects the decline of the economy, particularly for unskilled workers. The ratio of earnings relative to GDP per capita remained relatively constant for the period 1990-96. Loss of purchasing power can be reasonably blamed on a shrinking per capita economy. In the public sector over the same period, there has been a significant reduction in public sector wages relative to GDP per capita, except at entry level. This continues a dramatic long-term decline in earnings — at the middle levels of the civil service, monthly wages fell from US$602 in 1960 to US$78 in 1990, only to rise to US$82 in 1997. At the top of the civil service the decline is even more shocking: from US$900 a month in the early 1970s to US$321 in 1990, and US$170 in 1997.

Public Finances

Plagued by persistent revenue weaknesses, State finances were both a cause and a result of economic decline between 1991 and 1995. A cause, on one hand, since fiscal imbalances were the main source of uncontrolled monetary expansion; a result, on the other, due to the slow economic growth that affected the overall level of revenues. Fiscal deficits were in effect constantly worsening during the 1990-97 period. The efforts made for economic stabilization since 1995 have provoked a drastic compression of expenditures, only compensated by an increase in the external financing of capital expenditures. This was in part due to the populist policies during the 1993-94 period, which translated into massive tax exemptions on basic goods such as oil, rice, and flour. This also aggravated the deficit, bringing it to about 8 percent of GDP at end-1994. The financial stabilization of 1995 allowed the reorganization of finances at end-1996, with the deficit falling to less than 5 percent of GDP, a level at which it has remained in the last few years.

The public finances reorganization, in place since 1995 with improved fiscal revenue returns, has allowed the Government to re-establish its position vis-à-vis internal creditors, particularly the banking system. The debt-service relief granted during the Eighth Paris Club meeting in March 1997, together with the US$160 million balance-of-payment aid provided the same year by donors, constituted an exceptional deficit financing. The fiscal revenues level, which represents more than 80 percent of current revenues, was relatively weak during the 1990-97 period. Although fiscal revenues reached almost 15 percent of GDP in the early 1980s, this ratio fell by an average of 8 percentage points of GDP during the 1990-97 period.

The ratio of total public expenditure of GDP stabilized during the period 1990-97 at around 15 percent, except for the two years of macro-finance stabilization (1995-96) which had a 12 percent data record. Expenditures, in 1997 prices, increased by about 1 percent a year during the period, with a distribution of 55 percent for current expenditures and 45 percent for capital expenditures. The civil service wage bill and compensations accounted for almost half of the current expenditures, or 46 percent of the total. Wage bills in 1997 prices have decreased, and the purchase of goods and services to improve the efficiency of public administration has accounted for about 16 percent of current expenditures. Accounting for around 16 percent of current expenditures, transfers to public autonomous agencies and to local governments were in fact the only category of expenditures to register a substantial increase in real terms, having grown at an average annual rate of 13 percent. Since November 1995, the operational costs for newly created municipalities have been the main cause of this increase.

Debt servicing represents today 16 percent of current expenditures. Following the important reductions between 1993 and 1995, a period in which the country was unable to service its debt, the resources allocated to this category of expenditures registered from 1996 an important increase (in 1990 prices). The 1997 debt-service relief permitted the moderation of this increase in 1997. The average yearly growth established during the 1990-97 period was 6 percent for this category of expenditure.

Capital expenditures have mostly suffered from the weak increase in total revenues. With only 0.3 percent real growth since 1990, public investment is mainly covered by external financing, which represents in general more than 70 percent of expenditures. Despite insufficient internal financing to mobilize more external financing, the average Public Investment Program (PIP) percentage of execution during the period was around 80 percent, with a progressive level of realization due to the substantial improvement of the programming and monitoring exercises. This compares favorably with realization levels of 60 percent.

Graph A-1: Distribution per Sector of the Public Investment Program in 1990

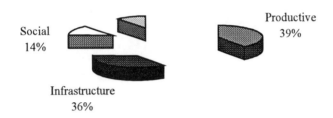

Source: INSTAT and World Bank.

Public investment is distributed among four main sectors. Financing to support the productive sector accounted for 32 percent of programmed capital expenditure, and infrastructure, social, and administrative sectors totaled 37 percent, 18 percent, and 12 percent of the PIP, respectively. The distribution of sectoral allocations also exhibited significant changes during the last few years. In 1990, support for the productive sector absorbed 40 percent of capital expenditures; its share had been reduced to 25 percent of the PIP by 1997. The share for the administrative sector registered a net decrease from 13 percent in 1991 to 8 percent of the PIP in 1997. This cut was in favor of the social and infrastructure sectors, which showed a respective share increase from 13 percent to 27 percent and from 35 percent to 40 percent between 1990 and 1997.

Graph A-2: Distribution per Sector of the Public Investment Program in 1997

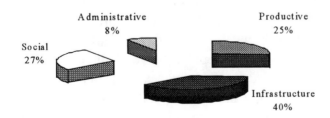

Source: Instat and World Bank.

External Sector

Madagascar has relied on commodities as a source of foreign exchange earnings. Although merchandise export volume rose at an average annual rate of 6.4 percent over the 1988-97 period, earnings have suffered from high variability owing to fluctuations in international market conditions. Prices for coffee, cloves, vanilla, and shellfish have dropped substantially over the past 10 years. To counter this uncertainty, Madagascar has diversified: only 43 percent of export earnings came from the four commodities in 1997, compared to 75 percent in 1988. Owing to this diversification, exports as a share of GDP rose from 12 percent in 1988 to 14 percent in 1997, reaching earnings of US$537 million, or about 70 percent of the merchandise import bill. Over the same period, imports have grown at an average annual rate of 6.3 percent in volume terms, while the terms of trade have deteriorated by 20 percent, or approximately 2 percent a year.

Graph A-3: Madagascar, Evolution of External Accounts

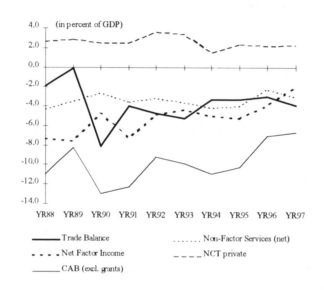

Source: Central Bank.

Despite the adverse movement in the terms of trade, Madagascar's economy has become more open. Merchandise exports and imports together comprised 27 percent of GDP in 1988, and increased to 36 percent of GDP in 1997 (see Figure A-3). Although fluctuations in the trade balance have existed in the late 1980s and very early 1990s, the period's ten-year average balance of -5.7 percent of GDP is representative of the trade balance in recent times. Madagascar's historical reliance on debt financing explains the country's high debt-service obligations, which reached 105 percent of exports (GNFS) in 1990, but dropped gradually to 42 percent in 1996. Debt-service obligations underlie the behavior of Madagascar's net factor income over the 1988-90 period. In 1988, interest obligations amounted to more than 7 percent of GDP. This ratio fell to around 2 percent of GDP in 1997. In contrast, Madagascar's net non-factor services were steady at about -4 percent of GDP through the 1988-97 period.

Madagascar's current account balance has been improving in recent years, reflecting better exchange rate and fiscal management. Figure A-3 provides an illustration, and indicates the extent to which movements in the trade balance and service payments are reflected in the CAB. Variability in the trade balance in 1989 and 1990, stemming from the expansive fiscal policies of the period and high interest payments in 1991 (at the time of the Paris Club rescheduling agreement), make up for the high current account balance of 1990-91, which was greater than 12 percent of GDP. Subsequent to 1991, both the trade balance and the service balance have remained rather stable, and the CAB in turn reflects the declining interest payment obligations.

Over the 1988-97 period, Madagascar has financed its current account deficit primarily by external grants, debt relief, and accumulation of arrears. Over the period, current and capital grants combined have amounted to approximately 5 percent of GDP, while arrears accumulation and debt relief together have amounted to 10 percent of GDP (see Figure A-4). The financing pattern remained stable during the period, with debt relief and the new accumulation of arrears alternating as a sizable financing source.

Graph A-4: Madagascar, External Financing

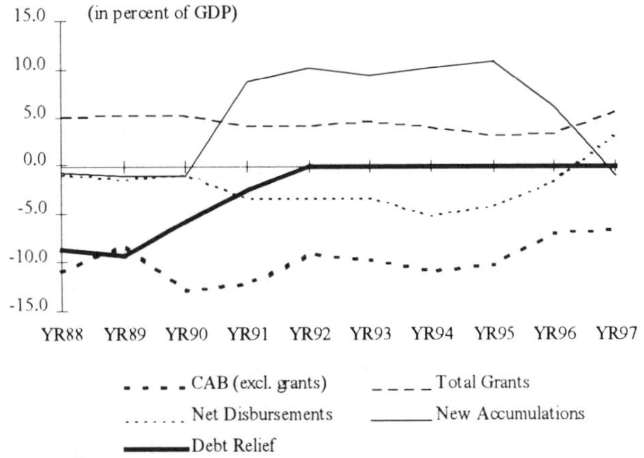

Source: Central Bank.

Money and Prices

Madagascar's monetary policy during the 1990s mirrors the country's struggle and success with stabilization in the late 1980s and 1990, the political events of 1991-93, and recourse to more consistent policy-making after the 1994/95 crisis. More specifically, during the late 1980s and early 1990s, the objective of monetary policy was to accommodate economic expansion while avoiding the pitfalls of domestic inflation and widening of the external current account. Late 1990 and 1991 saw a turnabout, owing to exogenous economic and political factors. Increased demand for imports due to the economic expansion and a drop in export prices put pressure on the country's current account, which deteriorated from 8.6 percent of GDP in 1990 to 11.7 percent in 1991, and reduced Madagascar's foreign reserves from five months to one month of imports. One of the remedies chosen was a 16 percent devaluation. Economic events, coupled with delays in the democratization process, led to political turmoil and a change in government, and resulted in the reversal of stabilization and adjustment policies.

The new national leadership's effort to reverse the economic decline of 1991, when GDP contracted by 6.3 percent, relied partially on simulative fiscal policy. As described above, the government deficit reached 6 percent of GDP in 1991 and 7 percent of GDP in 1992, financed primarily by foreign drawings and domestic credit. The banking system's credit to the government expanded by 30 percent in 1991 and by 121 percent in 1992. Concurrently, credit to the private sector, including public enterprises, grew at the rate of nominal GDP growth. The increase in domestic credit partially served to offset the loss of external reserves and to keep broad money growing at rates of earlier years, which averaged about 20 percent per annum for the period 1989-93.

Prices did not initially respond to changes in credit policies. The CPI for traditional items fluctuated between single and double digits over 1989-1993, ranging between 9 and 15 percent; the average annual change in the CPI was 10.8 percent, with a standard deviation of 2.8. The average annual change in the GDP deflator, a broader and more stable measure of prices, over 1989-93 was 12.5 percent, with a standard deviation of 0.9. The stability in the rate of change in the deflator, with declining rates of economic growth, implied a reduction in the velocity of money. However, as the government's expansive fiscal policy was sustained through 1994, inflation picked up and reached an annual rate of 62 percent at the end of 1994.

Madagascar's policy reversals toward protectionism and a government-run economy were short-lived. The government signed a Policy Framework Paper with the Bretton Woods institutions, reversing the policy setbacks instituted in 1992 and turning toward more responsible fiscal and monetary management. Since then the guiding principle behind monetary policy has been to eliminate excess liquidity, with the objective of reducing inflation and turning real interest rates positive. In terms of policy instruments, this was achieved by a thorough reduction in bank credit to the government, increases in reserves, and recovering outstanding loans for the two state banks. The net effect was a 15 percent increase in credit to the private sector, and a reduction of governed-sector credit by 3 percent in 1995. Broad money grew at 16 percent in 1995, compared to 48 percent in 1994. The measure, however, succeeded in curbing the annual inflation rate, which fell to 37 percent by December 1995. Continuous adherence to monetary discipline further succeeded in reducing the annual inflation rate to 9 percent by December 1996. Conservative fiscal policy through 1997, and a tight stance on monetizing the deficit (7 percent of GDP) contributed to holding inflation to 4.5 percent at end-1997.

Statistical Annex

Charts: Some Key Economic Indicators

Charts: Some Key Economic Indicators

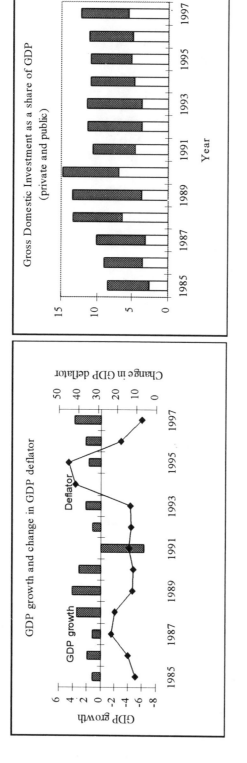

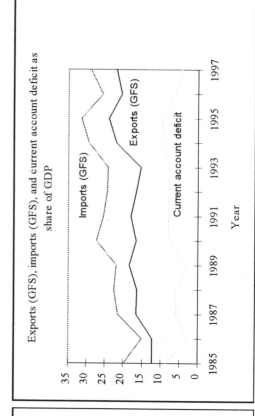

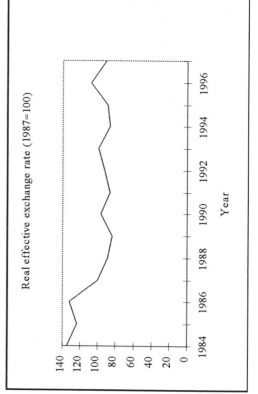

Source: IMF and World Bank.

60

Table 1: Summary of Macroeconomic Indicators

	1985	1986	1987	1988	1989	1990	1991	1992	1993	1994	1995	1996	1997
GDP growth	1.2%	2.0%	1.2%	3.4%	4.1%	3.1%	-6.3%	1.2%	2.1%	0.0%	1.7%	2.1%	3.6%
GDP inflation	10.4%	14.2%	23.0%	21.2%	12.0%	11.5%	13.9%	12.5%	13.0%	41.6%	45.2%	18.1%	7.4%
Investment growth	1.4%	5.3%	16.6%	33.9%	4.7%	28.0%	-56.6%	45.2%	8.7%	-14.3%	1.6%	9.4%	7.7%
Per capita private consumption growth	1.7%	-5.3%	-4.6%	-2.5%	-4.5%	0.9%	1.1%	-6.3%	-0.4%	13.2%	13.2%	-6.7%	5.4%
Export growth	-3.2%	0.0%	2.9%	-8.2%	16.9%	12.0%	4.8%	0.4%	5.4%	10.1%	3.3%	2.5%	5.5%
Import growth	24.1%	-20.9%	0.3%	-9.6%	0.9%	33.0%	-14.9%	1.5%	13.9%	0.4%	2.5%	0.3%	4.0%
(As a share of GDP)													
Resource balance	-7.7%	-2.9%	-4.9%	-6.2%	-3.6%	-10.7%	-7.5%	-7.9%	-8.9%	-7.5%	-7.3%	-5.3%	-7.0%
Exports GNFS	12.2%	12.1%	16.6%	16.3%	18.4%	16.6%	17.9%	16.5%	15.3%	22.0%	24.1%	20.5%	21.9%
Imports GNFS	19.9%	15.0%	21.5%	22.5%	22.0%	27.3%	25.4%	24.4%	24.2%	29.5%	31.5%	25.8%	28.9%
Invetsment	8.5%	9.0%	10.1%	13.3%	13.4%	14.8%	10.6%	11.3%	11.4%	10.9%	10.9%	11.1%	11.8%
Private	2.6%	3.6%	3.1%	6.4%	3.7%	6.9%	4.6%	3.7%	3.7%	4.7%	5.2%	5.0%	5.5%
Public	6.0%	5.4%	7.0%	6.9%	9.7%	7.9%	5.9%	7.6%	7.8%	6.2%	5.8%	6.2%	6.3%
Real effe. exch. rate (1987=100)	124	132	100	89	84	97	86	93	100	86	89	108	91
Export prices growth rate	-10.4%	17.1%	-10.3%	-5.4%	-9.1%	2.1%	-0.6%	-2.9%	-3.7%	20.6%	9.8%	-9.0%	-4.8%
Import prices growth rate	-5.8%	4.7%	16.8%	5.4%	-2.7%	12.2%	-2.3%	3.5%	-4.6%	4.7%	8.3%	0.1%	-7.4%
Terms of trade	95	107	82	74	69	63	64	60	60	69	70	64	66
Offic. foreign reserves (in weeks of GFS)	4.2	4.1	2.2	1.9	1.9	5.4	6.6	6.1	5.2	3.6	5.9	12.3	13.7
Cur. acount balance/GDP (after curr. grants)	-8.7%	-3.0%	-5.7%	-5.8%	-3.0%	-7.7%	-8.1%	-7.4%	-7.8%	-9.5%	-9.7%	-6.2%	-4.4%
Fiscal deficit (before grants)	-4.3%	-4.2%	-4.0%	-4.1%	-8.2%	-5.1%	-7.7%	-10.1%	-10.7%	-11.4%	-9.1%	-9.1%	-7.7%
Fiscal deficit (after grants)	-3.9%	-3.5%	-3.4%	-3.3%	-4.1%	-0.7%	-5.5%	-6.6%	-7.2%	-8.4%	-6.2%	-4.9%	-2.4%
Growth of money supply	13%	24%	18%	20%	30%	0%	25%	20%	26%	49%	16%	18%	25%
Memorandum:													
Exchange rate (FMG/$US average)	662	676	1069	1407	1603	1494	1835	1864	1914	3083	4268	4055	5090
GDP (in $US)	2858	3258	2566	2442	2498	3081	2677	3001	3370	2962	3158	4006	3622
Population (in million)	10.0	10.3	10.6	11.0	11.3	11.7	11.9	12.2	12.6	12.9	13.3	13.7	14.1

Source: INSTAT, IMF, and World Bank.

Table 2: GDP by Sectors In Current Prices, 1984-1997
In billions of FMG

	1984	1985	1986	1987	1988	1989	1990	1991	1992	1993	1994	1995	1996*	1997**
PRIMARY SECTOR	531.0	592.7	729.5	865.9	1,020.6	1,200.4	1,357.1	1,508.2	1,727.1	2,041.1	3,342.6	4,109.3	4,807.5	5,319.2
Agriculture	277.7	316.8	373.2	461.3	576.4	634.1	700.6	772.8	809.6	978.2	2019.6	2571.6	2686.0	2937.1
Livestock, Fisheries	200.7	209.4	244.6	268.3	344.2	394.5	460.1	517.7	636.8	737.0	886.5	1008.8	1360.3	1465.9
Forestry	52.5	66.5	111.7	136.3	99.9	171.7	196.3	217.7	280.7	325.9	436.5	528.9	761.2	916.2
SECONDARY SECTOR	195.0	224.6	255.0	328.1	401.2	538.7	599.3	648.1	715.5	832.9	1,155.1	1,716.9	2,047.6	2,351.3
Agro-indus.	14.8	16.2	25.5	29.8	48.9	72.1	68.5	59.0	56.9	47.3	76.4	125.8	150.5	155.0
Mining	2.8	4.5	5.3	8.1	14.6	16.3	22.1	18.6	19.0	18.2	25.5	52.5	45.3	67.4
Energy	19.2	26.3	26.9	33.4	46.8	43.4	57.3	70.3	81.9	99.9	101.0	159.3	207.0	253.3
Food	41.4	50.7	61.3	84.7	47.3	96.7	106.4	130.5	148.8	170.6	224.0	336.1	436.7	479.8
Beverage	10.9	14.0	16.9	35.8	61.2	72.5	87.4	97.0	106.8	121.6	204.9	287.8	347.1	379.0
Tabacco	12.9	15.4	16.5	18.3	23.1	27.3	24.9	26.3	34.4	39.4	45.0	52.6	104.2	90.5
Edible Oil and Fats	8.1	7.3	8.2	22.0	21.2	25.2	27.4	31.8	31.7	33.3	34.2	61.1	61.5	62.5
Chemical and Pharmaceutical	8.4	9.5	7.4	17.7	21.8	23.0	24.6	26.9	34.4	50.3	86.0	113.2	121.3	143.2
Textiles	25.8	24.3	33.3	42.2	43.8	65.6	63.3	45.9	44.9	50.1	65.8	60.1	44.5	49.0
Leather	5.5	6.1	9.2	6.3	4.9	8.2	9.9	6.6	6.0	5.7	7.1	7.7	8.5	9.2
Wood Industries	3.8	4.0	6.2	3.7	4.9	7.5	8.6	9.5	12.3	14.3	19.1	29.0	41.8	49.0
Construction Materials	4.8	3.8	11.9	13.1	12.3	10.5	16.7	18.9	21.4	27.1	33.8	46.9	54.1	68.0
Metal Industries	5.2	4.3	5.6	9.1	14.7	15.6	20.3	14.3	16.5	23.6	34.5	66.8	83.7	95.8
Transport Materials	4.3	5.0	2.9	5.6	5.8	6.8	7.1	6.8	10.0	9.1	16.5	22.7	28.9	33.4
Electronical Industries	12.0	13.0	19.0	20.6	21.5	22.2	27.5	60.5	49.0	67.6	75.3	102.4	116.7	157.7
Paper and Printing	10.6	13.1	13.8	12.5	17.3	21.3	23.8	16.9	23.8	22.7	47.4	60.4	36.9	50.7
Others Industries	4.6	7.1	-14.8	-34.9	-8.8	4.5	3.7	4.1	7.8	4.7	15.0	5.4	11.5	12.3
Export Processing Zone (EPZ)							0.0	4.2	9.9	27.4	43.5	127.0	147.3	195.6
TERTIARY SECTOR	636.5	730.9	853.2	979.4	1,264.5	1,963.2	2,310.1	2,477.5	2,808.3	3,221.6	4,202.5	6,885.3	8,449.5	9,619.7
Construction	14.4	17.7	27.2	29.0	44.5	49.5	65.4	54.5	66.8	77.0	106.2	170.3	222.2	296.8
Transport (merchandise)	151.3	192.1	229.1	257.8	340.0	410.4	503.6	502.7	591.5	703.2	884.8	1477.4	1695.7	2048.6
Transport (passengers)	35.5	40.2	48.1	65.0	93.4	113.0	130.3	127.5	156.6	177.8	264.2	486.6	550.4	582.7
Transport-related service	43.3	62.8	74.9	90.7	119.6	143.2	164.6	164.3	193.3	229.8	289.2	483.8	554.2	624.8
Telecommunications	7.3	9.6	10.8	13.2	18.1	26.8	38.6	46.4	54.5	59.9	65.9	68.2	86.0	103.6
Commerce	194.0	199.7	233.4	237.0	303.8	357.2	398.8	449.4	525.2	594.1	797.2	1359.0	2085.0	2357.4
Banking	28.9	29.3	31.8	43.2	49.1	56.5	64.7	59.7	67.1	77.2	102.5	147.4	211.9	162.1
Insurance	0.7	1.0	1.1	0.9	1.1	9.4	11.7	12.7	13.3	15.2	19.4	29.0	38.6	44.5
Services	53.4	61.0	71.3	90.5	116.1	603.2	687.6	772.1	834.9	946.6	1252.4	2089.8	2326.9	2539.6
Public Administration	107.8	117.6	125.5	152.1	178.9	193.9	244.8	288.2	305.1	340.8	420.7	573.7	678.6	835.4
Imputed bank service charge (less)	-29.5	-29.9	-32.4	-44.0	-50.1	-57.7	-66.1	-61.0	-68.5	-79.3	-129.3	-186.0	-195.4	-207.8
GDP at Factor Cost	1,362.5	1,548.3	1,837.8	2,173.4	2,686.3	3,702.4	4,266.5	4,633.7	5,250.9	6,095.6	8,700.1	12,525.6	15,304.6	17,290.2
Net Indirect taxes	190.4	206.7	220.7	349.5	389.0	360.7	403.6	340.9	410.7	434.6	560.3	953.2	1116.2	1354.7
GDP at Market Price (w/o EPZ)	1,695.0	1,893.2	2,203.7	2,743.1	3,436.8	4,005.4	4,604.1	4,909.5	5,583.1	6,423.5	9,087.6	13,478.8	16,225.4	18,437.2
GDP at Market Price (with EPZ)	1,695.0	1,893.2	2,203.7	2,743.1	3,436.8	4,005.4	4,604.1	4,913.7	5,593.1	6,450.9	9,131.1	13,605.8	16,372.7	18,632.8

*Estimates **Provisional

Source: Ministry of Finance and INSTAT.

Table 3: GDP by Sectors in Constant 1984 Prices, 1984-1997

In billions of FMG

	1984	1985	1986	1987	1988	1989	1990	1991	1992	1993	1994	1995	1996*	1997**
PRIMARY SECTOR	531.0	536.9	554.3	568.2	580.7	610.9	623.6	626.8	637.5	658.0	655.0	667.3	684.0	700.0
Agriculture	277.7	273.7	277.4	282.8	281.9	300.0	302.7	300.0	303.6	317.0	303.3	307.6	315.2	320.4
Livestock, Fisheries	200.7	211.0	223.3	232.0	244.5	257.1	265.3	268.0	272.0	275.9	280.4	286.0	291.0	296.0
Forestry	52.5	52.2	53.5	53.4	54.2	53.8	55.6	58.8	61.9	65.1	71.3	73.7	77.7	83.6
SECONDARY SECTOR (calculé)	195.0	197.6	205.1	214.8	218.6	221.3	219.9	219.1	216.8	223.8	221.5	225.4	229.8	238.0
Agro-industries	14.8	15.0	14.9	16.3	18.5	19.4	17.8	14.7	12.4	9.7	10.8	12.3	12.0	11.2
Mining	2.8	3.8	3.5	3.3	4.4	4.3	4.3	3.7	3.9	4.4	4.2	4.8	4.5	4.9
Energy	19.2	24.7	25.2	26.4	28.8	26.4	27.8	33.5	37.1	40.4	31.5	34.1	36.9	40.8
Food	41.4	40.9	41.4	42.2	42.1	44.8	45.2	44.8	45.3	47.3	47.2	47.4	48.6	47.5
Beverage	10.9	12.0	12.2	17.4	22.4	22.4	25.9	21.5	21.6	21.6	23.3	27.8	30.6	38.1
Tabacco	12.9	12.7	13.6	13.2	13.1	12.9	11.0	10.8	11.7	11.8	11.2	9.9	15.6	11.5
Edible Oil and Fats	8.1	7.2	8.2	14.4	12.5	12.6	12.4	12.9	12.1	12.2	9.8	11.0	9.3	9.0
Chemical and Pharmaceutical	8.4	9.0	6.6	10.7	11.2	10.4	9.9	9.2	9.9	10.6	11.2	9.3	9.6	10.5
Textiles	25.8	24.3	24.4	24.0	22.4	23.5	21.2	19.7	17.9	18.0	18.3	12.7	7.0	7.0
Leather	5.5	5.9	7.9	4.6	2.7	4.4	5.7	4.2	4.0	4.1	4.1	3.3	3.2	1.4
Wood Industries	3.8	3.3	4.1	3.3	4.1	4.8	4.9	5.2	5.5	5.8	6.3	6.6	6.9	6.5
Construction Materials	4.8	4.0	6.8	6.0	4.9	3.6	4.1	4.3	4.5	5.0	4.6	5.1	5.0	5.9
Metal Industries	5.2	3.8	3.9	4.3	3.9	4.0	3.5	2.9	2.9	3.8	4.4	5.8	5.8	6.1
Transport Materials	4.3	4.3	2.4	4.0	4.1	4.3	4.0	3.3	4.0	3.2	4.2	4.0	4.1	4.3
Electronical Industries	12.0	11.0	12.9	11.1	10.1	9.4	9.4	19.7	11.6	13.7	13.1	13.0	12.2	14.3
Paper and Printing	10.6	11.3	11.5	8.7	9.5	10.8	10.4	5.5	6.4	5.7	7.6	7.2	4.2	3.8
Others Industries	4.6	4.5	5.7	4.9	3.9	3.4	2.5	2.5	4.3	2.3	5.4	1.0	1.8	1.7
EPZ							0.0	0.8	1.7	4.4	4.1	10.1	12.6	13.5
TERTIARY SECTOR	808.1	815.1	820.7	819.3	855.6	890.7	925.8	854.3	863.9	882.3	892.7	906.4	925.6	965.1
Construction	14.4	15.9	19.6	17.4	19.1	20.1	23.6	17.6	22.2	22.1	22.9	26.3	28.1	31.2
Transport (merchandise)	151.3	152.5	157.3	159.2	169.3	177.7	188.3	168.0	181.4	186.8	186.4	186.4	192.6	213.2
Transport (passengers)	35.5	33.8	32.7	35.0	39.0	42.7	45.4	38.2	40.3	44.3	47.4	52.0	59.8	61.0
Transport-related service	43.3	45.4	46.9	47.4	50.4	52.9	56.1	50.0	54.0	55.6	55.5	55.6	57.4	59.2
Telecommunications	7.3	8.3	8.7	9.4	10.0	10.7	11.8	13.3	15.1	16.6	18.3	18.9	23.8	26.4
Commerce	194.0	193.5	192.6	195.7	201.6	216.4	221.9	210.0	203.4	206.2	209.0	212.8	219.8	226.3
Banking	28.9	27.1	27.7	31.4	30.6	32.5	33.1	24.6	24.7	24.9	25.3	25.7	26.1	26.6
Insurance	0.7	0.9	0.9	0.6	0.6	0.7	0.8	0.7	0.6	0.6	0.7	0.7	0.7	0.7
Services	224.9	229.1	225.0	213.7	225.3	227.3	233.9	221.3	212.9	216.0	219.0	222.3	209.2	212.4
Public Administration	107.8	108.7	109.4	109.5	109.6	109.6	110.9	110.6	109.3	109.1	108.1	105.7	108.1	108.1
Imputed bank service charge (less)	-29.5	-27.7	-28.2	-32.0	-31.3	-33.2	-33.8	-25.1	-25.2	-25.4	-31.5	-32.0	-32.5	-33.1
GDP at Factor Cost	1504.6	1521.9	1551.9	1570.2	1623.6	1689.8	1735.6	1675.1	1693.0	1738.7	1737.7	1767.1	1807.0	1870.0
Net Indirect taxes	190.4	192.7	196.3	198.6	205.4	213.8	227.6	164.2	168.1	161.4	161.6	164.2	165.8	174.9
GDP at Market Price (w/o EPZ)	1695.0	1714.6	1748.2	1768.8	1829.0	1903.6	1963.2	1838.5	1859.4	1895.7	1895.1	1921.3	1960.2	2031.5
GDP at Market Price (with EPZ)	1695.0	1714.6	1748.2	1768.8	1829.0	1903.6	1963.2	1839.3	1861.1	1900.1	1899.2	1931.3	1972.8	2044.9

Source: Ministry of Finance and INSTAT.

* Estimates   ** Provisional

Table 4: GDP by Expenditure Categories at Current Prices
In billions of FMG

	1984	1985	1986	1987	1988	1989	1990	1991	1992	1993	1994	1995	1996*	1997**
GDP at Market Price	1695.0	1893.2	2203.8	2745.4	3439.2	4005.3	4604.1	4914.4	5593.1	6451.1	9131.6	13478.8	16225.4	18437.2
Import of Goods and Non-Factor Services (net)	78.4	156.5	74.9	163.0	233.7	153.1	526.0	417.7	467.0	600.6	705.5	856.3	895.1	1350.9
Imports	303.6	388.3	342.6	617.4	793.9	892.0	1290.4	1299.6	1390.6	1587.9	2715.1	4274.3	4222.1	5555.4
Exports	225.1	231.8	267.7	454.4	560.2	738.9	764.4	881.8	923.6	987.3	2009.6	3418.0	3327.0	4204.5
Available Resources	1773.4	2049.7	2278.7	2908.3	3672.9	4158.4	5130.1	5332.1	6060.0	7051.7	9836.6	14335.0	17120.5	19788.1
Consumption	1627.3	1887.9	2079.5	2631.1	3216.0	3622.1	4348.7	4930.7	5428.2	6313.2	8841.0	12860.1	15311.2	17507.0
Government	166.8	184.8	194.9	250.5	279.6	350.9	367.3	422.0	463.4	506.5	628.8	904.2	1048.7	1346.2
Private	1460.5	1703.1	1884.6	2380.6	2936.4	3271.2	3981.4	4508.7	4964.8	5806.7	8212.2	11955.9	14262.4	16160.8
Gross Domestic Investment	146.1	161.8	199.2	277.2	456.9	536.3	781.4	401.4	631.9	738.5	995.6	1474.9	1809.3	2281.1
Public	108.9	112.9	119.5	191.6	237.3	388.1	365.2	291.6	423.9	500.8	565.6	779.9	1003.1	1023.9
Private	37.2	48.9	79.7	85.6	219.6	148.2	317.0	227.3	207.9	237.7	430.0	695.0	806.2	1023.9
Change in Stock							99.2	-117.5						
Gross Domestic Saving	67.7	5.3	124.3	114.3	223.2	383.2	255.4	-16.4	164.9	137.9	290.1	618.8	914.3	930.2

Source: INSTAT.

*Estimates
**Provisional

Table 5: GDP by Expenditure Categories at Constant 1984 Prices
In billions of FMG

	1984	1985	1986	1987	1988	1989	1990	1991	1992	1993	1994	1995	1996*	1997**
GDP at Market Price	1695.0	1714.6	1748.2	1768.7	1829.0	1903.5	1963.1	1839.3	1861.0	1900.1	1899.3	1931.2	1971.2	2044.13
GDP Growth Rate		1.2%	2.0%	1.2%	3.4%	4.1%	3.1%	-6.3%	1.2%	2.1%	0.0%	1.7%	2.1%	3.6%
Imports of Goods (net)	47.2	119.5	49.5	44.1	36.8	4.4	56.1	-4.6	-1.7	22.0	-6.5	-9.3	-16.6	-22.6
Imports	270.3	335.5	265.4	266.2	240.6	242.7	322.9	274.9	279.0	317.9	319.2	327.2	328.3	341.3
Exports	223.1	216.0	215.9	222.1	203.8	238.3	266.8	279.5	280.7	295.9	325.7	336.5	344.9	363.9
Available Resources	1742.2	1834.1	1797.7	1812.8	1865.8	1907.9	2019.2	1834.7	1859.3	1922.1	1892.8	1921.9	1954.6	2021.6
Consumption	1596.2	1686.1	1641.8	1631.1	1622.4	1653.0	1692.8	1693.0	1653.6	1698.4	1701.0	1727.1	1741.4	1785.8
Government	166.8	170.9	169.9	182.0	174.3	184.2	179.2	166.8	164.1	161.6	153.6	157.8	154.5	166.9
Private	1429.4	1515.2	1471.9	1449.1	1448.1	1468.8	1513.6	1526.2	1489.5	1536.8	1547.4	1569.3	1586.9	1618.9
Gross Domestic Investment	146.0	148.0	155.9	181.8	243.4	254.9	326.4	141.7	205.7	223.7	191.8	194.8	213.2	235.8
Public	108.8	103.3	93.5	125.6	126.4	184.5	152.5	102.9	138.0	151.7	108.9	102.9	116.7	127.2
Private	37.2	44.7	62.4	56.2	117.0	70.4	173.9	38.8	67.7	72.0	82.9	91.8	96.5	108.6
Change in Stock														
Gross Domestic Saving	98.8	28.5	106.4	137.6	206.6	250.5	270.3	146.3	207.4	201.7	198.3	204.1	229.8	258.4
GDP Growth Rate		1.2%	2.0%	1.2%	3.4%	4.1%	3.1%	-6.3%	1.2%	2.1%	0.0%	1.7%	2.1%	3.6%
Consumption as share of GDP	94.2%	98.3%	93.9%	92.2%	88.7%	86.8%	86.2%	92.0%	88.9%	89.4%	89.6%	89.4%	88.3%	87.4%
Investment as share of GDP	8.6%	8.6%	8.9%	10.3%	13.3%	13.4%	16.6%	7.7%	11.1%	11.8%	10.1%	10.1%	10.8%	11.5%
Dom. Saving as share of GDP	5.8%	1.7%	6.1%	7.8%	11.3%	13.2%	13.8%	8.0%	11.1%	10.6%	10.4%	10.6%	11.7%	12.6%

Source: INSTAT and World Bank staff estimates.

*Estimates
**Provisional

Table 6: Consumer Price Index, 1984-1996
August 1971-July 1972=100, Traditional*

	1984	1985	1986	1987	1988	1989	1990	1991	1992	1993	1994	1995	1996
January	479.3	531.4	618.6	668.3	900.6	968.4	1,092.2	1,169.3	1,347.3	1,518.4	1,746.0	2,691.3	3,674.1
February	486.6	543.2	633.0	667.1	897.0	960.1	1,095.8	1,189.1	1,355.4	1,513.4	1,922.3	2,770.1	3,748.4
March	495.7	543.2	626.6	667.6	809.5	986.1	1,115.9	1,198.0	1,404.2	1,529.8	1,982.0	2,934.4	3,833.8
April	482.5	541.4	609.4	668.2	913.3	966.2	1,113.5	1,203.1	1,328.7	1,506.2	1,802.9	2,957.8	3,864.7
May	481.4	532.9	600.7	671.1	912.8	970.1	1,095.5	1,178.6	1,326.1	1,490.8	1,859.3	2,986.8	3,819.5
June	490.4	535.9	609.3	677.5	916.3	976.0	1,101.4	1,188.4	1,356.9	1,480.8	2,019.8	3,105.2	3,786.0
July	492.7	538.7	622.0	690.5	913.4	998.4	1,107.0	1,193.4	1,372.7	1,471.3	2,049.8	3,223.9	3,751.7
August	500.6	551.7	644.4	711.0	914.4	1,009.6	1,124.5	1,212.0	1,404.7	1,512.8	2,114.6	3,302.7	3,758.2
September	507.0	560.0	647.2	759.2	928.9	1,031.9	1,136.4	1,241.1	1,440.1	1,554.0	2,350.8	3,469.1	3,802.9
October	515.0	566.1	651.8	828.9	935.1	1,051.3	1,158.9	1,271.8	1,443.5	1,593.5	2,504.8	3,535.6	3,868.9
November	520.1	576.6	653.5	849.7	937.7	1,052.8	1,157.8	1,267.1	1,451.7	1,611.7	2,606.2	3,548.7	3,858.9
December	532.6	594.6	658.3	886.2	971.1	1,074.1	1,166.1	1,309.9	1,512.3	1,637.1	2,639.3	3,624.0	3,924.2
Average Year Index	498.7	551.3	631.2	728.8	912.5	1,003.8	1,122.1	1,218.5	1,395.3	1,535.0	2,133.2	3,179.1	3,807.6
Average Year Rate		10.6	14.5	15.5	25.2	10.0	11.8	8.6	14.5	10.0	39.0	49.0	19.8

Large groups of Products: Food: 60.4%
Types of Products: Local Products: 49.2%

Source: Central Bank and Ministry of Finance.

66

Table 7: Consumer Price Index, 1984-1996
August 1971-July 1972=100, Modern*

	1984	1985	1986	1987	1988	1989	1990	1991	1992	1993	1994	1995	1996
January	434.9	486.2	522.7	591.8	826.5	909.1	1,030.1	1,151.8	1,255.0	1,394.7	1,540.3	2,268.0	3,149.9
February	438.7	488.9	532.5	605.7	843.1	914.3	1,039.7	1,170.1	1,266.2	1,392.8	1,582.5	2,315.0	3,183.1
March	439.9	491.9	535.0	619.1	850.4	959.2	1,057.1	1,176.2	1,277.6	1,421.1	1,618.5	2,502.1	3,275.3
April	443.5	491.7	534.1	632.8	857.1	954.6	1,058.5	1,180.0	1,281.4	1,421.3	1,631.5	2,594.7	3,296.7
May	445.5	489.2	537.6	639.3	858.5	955.6	1,053.6	1,187.8	1,289.5	1,419.4	1,675.9	2,627.7	3,316.1
June	454.2	490.4	537.5	640.4	875.9	953.0	1,066.2	1,185.3	1,285.6	1,431.5	1,880.5	2,757.8	3,326.0
July	462.9	493.0	538.8	655.2	877.0	954.4	1,082.3	1,189.1	1,282.3	1,438.4	1,918.9	2,845.4	3,334.4
August	470.9	494.6	540.7	679.5	884.5	958.4	1,079.1	1,195.0	1,297.6	1,444.2	1,944.3	2,899.6	3,336.4
September	474.7	498.9	547.7	729.1	893.8	972.2	1,127.7	1,208.8	1,323.4	1,453.7	2,109.5	2,972.7	3,371.3
October	475.9	499.2	568.0	792.0	893.3	1,000.9	1,133.1	1,218.0	1,337.9	1,458.9	2,161.2	3,002.2	3,370.6
November	479.4	501.8	568.5	805.8	899.0	1,004.9	1,131.5	1,215.7	1,334.9	1,464.3	2,175.1	3,041.0	3,384.0
December	481.1	502.5	584.0	815.1	905.4	1,009.3	1,142.8	1,233.6	1,368.3	1,475.6	2,223.0	3,098.4	3,419.7
Average Year Index	458.5	494.0	545.6	683.8	872.0	962.2	1,083.5	1,192.6	1,300.0	1,434.7	1,871.8	2,743.7	3,313.6
Average Year Rate		7.8	10.4	25.3	27.5	10.3	12.6	10.1	9.0	10.4	30.5	46.6	20.8

Large groups of Products: Food: 45%
Types of Products: Local Products: 15.5%

Source: Central Bank and Ministry of Finance.

67

Table 8: Summary Balance of Payments, 1988-1997
(In millions of SDRs)

	1988	1989	1990	1991	1992	1993	1994	1995	1996*	1997**
Trade balance	-35.1	-1.7	-183.4	-77.8	-100.2	-127.1	-68.6	-69.4	-83.4	-103.7
Exports, f.o.b.	208.1	248.1	234.1	243.9	230.1	237.9	312.4	344.6	360.6	369.4
Imports, f.o.b.	-243.3	-249.9	-417.5	-321.7	-330.3	-365.0	-381.0	-414.0	-444.0	-473.1
Services (net)	-211.6	-215.2	-167.2	-210.9	-173.1	-193.1	-189.9	-193.4	-171.6	-131.7
Service receipts	98.0	125.7	154.0	110.3	125.7	133.9	145.1	162.1	210.7	214.3
Service payments	-309.6	-340.9	-321.2	-321.2	-298.8	-327.0	-335.0	-355.5	-382.2	-346.0
Freight and insurance	-29.1	-29.8	-44.7	-36.9	-48.7	-58.0	-61.2	-67.5	-72.4	-75.6
Transport and travel	-65.4	-59.9	-67.9	-62.5	-65.9	-57.6	-68.7	-77.3	-86.9	-92.6
Investment income	-143.2	-161.4	-118.3	-145.2	-108.7	-107.2	-105.6	-114.5	-114.9	-59.6
Of which: public interest payments	-142.7	-160.9	-106.0	-134.3	-100.4	-99.0	-99.9	-108.2	-111.1	-52.3
Other	-71.9	-89.8	-90.3	-76.6	-75.5	-104.2	-99.5	-96.2	-108.0	-118.1
Private unrequited transfers (net)	47.7	55.9	56.7	48.8	77.4	81.8	32.1	49.5	60.7	60.0
Current account balance, excluding net official transfers	-199.0	-161.0	-293.9	-239.9	-195.9	-238.5	-226.5	-213.3	-194.3	-175.4
In percent of GDP	-11.0	-8.3	-12.9	-12.3	-9.2	-9.9	-10.9	-10.2	-7.0	-6.7
Public unrequited transfers (net)	92.9	102.5	118.4	82.3	89.4	112.2	81.0	67.0	91.0	147.6
Current grants	92.9	102.5	118.4	82.3	38.5	49.8	30.9	11.2	22.6	59.1
Balance of payments grants	13.0	27.2	33.0	23.2	12.8	20.3	8.9	1.7	8.5	65.7
Other current grants, net 1/	79.9	75.3	85.4	59.1	25.7	29.5	22.0	9.5	14.1	-6.6
Project grants					50.9	62.4	50.1	55.8	68.4	88.5
Current account balance, including net official transfers	-106.1	-58.5	-175.5	-157.6	-106.5	-126.3	-145.5	-146.3	-103.3	-27.7
In percent of GDP	-5.8	-3.0	-7.7	-8.1	-5.0	-5.2	-7.0	-7.0	-3.7	-1.1
Capital account	12.9	-76.9	-32.8	-46.6	-99.7	-92.3	-69.6	-37.0	26.5	85.9
Non-monetary capital (net)	-16.3	-35.9	-19.9	-72.7	-79.6	-89.8	-107.5	-92.5	-52.7	78.9
Drawings	147.5	149.6	110.3	131.8	88.2	87.8	55.5	60.1	62.0	158.2
Of which: private drawings										
public project loans										
public program loans										
Amortization	-149.6	-166.4	-131.4	-198.1	-159.6	-166.8	-159.6	-147.4	-108.7	-74.5
Of which: public sector										
Long-term liabilities (net)	0.0	-7.6	1.2	-6.4	-8.2	-10.8	-3.4	-5.2	-6.0	-4.8
Petroleum financing	-14.2	-11.5								
Drawing	11.5	0.0								
Amortization	-25.7	-11.5								
Commercial banks (net)	-0.8	-14.5	14.0	-17.4	-11.3	-16.3	-6.7	-14.9	25.3	-3.0
Direct investment	0.0	10.0	16.5	10.0	15.0	11.0	4.0	6.4	7.0	10.0
Other (incl. errors & omissions)	30.0	-36.5	-43.4	33.5	-23.9	2.8	40.6	64.0	46.9	0.0
Overall balance	-93.2	-135.4	-208.3	-204.2	-206.3	-218.6	-215.1	-183.3	-76.8	58.2
Financing	93.2	135.4	208.3	204.2	206.3	218.6	215.1	183.3	76.8	-58.2
Net foreign assets (increase -)	-66.9	-46.7	79.6	79.8	-101.7	-13.1	6.7	-39.8	-92.6	-31.9
Use of Fund credit (net)	-21.7	-12.9	-21.8	-11.9	-11.5	-10.1	-8.2	-9.4	1.9	0.7
Purchase	7.8									
Repurchases	-29.5	-38.3	-34.7	-25.0	-11.5	-7.4	-4.5	-0.6		
SAF/ESAF (net)		25.4	12.9	13.1		-2.7	-3.7	-8.8	1.9	0.7
Change in CBM arrears (increase +)	-15.3	-20.6	-21.7	92.1	-89.6	-1.4	0.4			
Other assets, net (increase -)	-29.9	-13.2	123.1	-0.3	-0.6	-1.6	14.5	-30.4	-94.5	-32.5
Net change in arrears (excl. CBM)	2.6	-0.6	-2.6	76.8	305.2	227.9	208.4	223.1	169.3	-1473.5
Debt relief and cancellation	157.5	182.6	131.3	47.6	2.8	3.7	0.0	0.0	0.0	1447.1
Official creditors	157.5	178.3	126.1	47.6	2.8	3.7				
Commercial banks	0.0	4.3	5.2							

* : Estimates
** : Provisional

Source: Central Bank and IMF.

Table 9: Merchandise Exports, 1984-1997

In Millions of SDR, Volume in metric tons, Unit Price in SDR/Kg

		1984	1985	1986	1987	1988	1989	1990	1991	1992	1993	1994	1995	1996*	1997**
Coffee	Price	137.640	101.400	118.790	71.660	54.810	59.900	28.460	20.520	22.420	28.980	59.880	61.160	42.600	31.060
	Volume	53,780	44,700	47,110	47,457	43,106	61,641	47,824	40,878	49,448	50,918	40,646	39,207	44,170	35,700
	Unit Price	2.559	2.268	2.522	1.510	1.272	0.972	0.595	0.502	0.453	0.569	1.473	1.560	0.960	0.870
Vanilla	Price	51.340	43.000	40.750	68.660	32.440	32.820	42.070	34.070	36.670	24.640	44.250	27.220	13.510	13.800
	Volume	830	630	687	1,261	625	595	829	642	700	485	1,066	750	1,160	1,200
	Unit Price	61.855	68.254	59.316	54.449	51.904	55.160	50.748	53.069	51.950	50.804	41.510	36.290	11.610	11.500
Cloves	Price	35.690	34.700	23.480	7.730	11.550	25.080	14.750	16.860	6.390	4.510	5.870	7.220	3.630	5.100
	Volume	6,270	11,530	10,180	3,005	5,374	16,449	10,222	13,084	10,585	11,358	17,118	17,127	7,070	10,000
	Unit Price	5.692	3.010	2.306	2.572	2.149	1.525	1.443	1.289	0.604	0.397	0.343	0.420	0.510	0.510
Pepper	Price	3.910	5.140	4.470	4.870	5.480	2.440	1.520	1.800	1.590	1.690	2.130	1.970	2.750	2.040
	Volume	2,800	2,620	1,840	1,851	2,497	1,417	1,222	1,844	1,948	2,000	2,282	1,439	1,860	1,200
	Unit Price	1.396	1.962	2.429	2.631	2.195	1.722	1.244	0.976	0.816	0.845	0.933	1.360	1.480	1.700
Shrimps	Price	21.310	21.750	21.040	26.370	22.660	23.760	24.850	29.890	26.900	28.620	40.430	38.790	43.640	44.850
	Volume	3,800	4,260	4,270	5,143	5,091	5,309	5,085	6,589	5,891	6,915	7,724	8,200	8,030	7,500
	Unit Price	5.608	5.106	4.927	5.127	4.451	4.475	4.887	4.536	4.566	4.139	5.234	4.730	5.430	5.980
Sugar	Price	9.190	9.350	0.000	6.560	6.500	18.800	12.260	7.510	6.550	4.630	6.930	9.360	11.450	13.260
	Volume	28,080	32,800	0	18,611	18,990	72,127	38,680	21,129	17,238	11,266	23,096	22,274	25,650	26,000
	Unit Price	0.327	0.285	0.350	0.352	0.342	0.261	0.317	0.355	0.380	0.411	0.300	0.420	0.450	0.510
Meat	Price	4.130	1.580	0.140	0.230	0.250	0.200	0.150	0.610	2.070	0.770	3.880	5.800	2.730	0.990
	Volume	3,490	1,270	100	159	219	150	114	392	1,293	1,720	2,779	3,790	1,760	720
	Unit Price	1.183	1.244	1.430	1.447	1.142	1.333	1.316	1.556	1.601	1.610	1.396	1.530	1.550	1.370
Cocoa	Price	4.430	2.900	3.090	3.380	4.060	1.750	1.810	2.900	1.780	2.560	1.910	2.600	2.280	0.900
	Volume	2,500	1,620	2,120	2,963	3,691	2,384	2,590	4,273	2,730	4,079	2,226	3,256	2,900	1,050
	Unit Price	1.772	1.790	1.458	1.141	1.100	0.734	0.699	0.679	0.652	0.628	0.858	0.800	0.790	0.860
Textile	Price	10.990	12.220	6.530	9.390	9.710	10.390	6.340	9.990	6.740	5.170	9.270	7.390	7.080	9.140
	Volume	4,450	4,690	2,840	4,589	4,861	4,553	2,418	4,048	2,634	2,050	2,432	2,008	1,490	2,000
	Unit Price	2.470	2.606	2.299	2.046	1.998	2.282	2.622	2.468	2.559	2.522	3.812	3.680	4.770	4.570
Sisal	Price	4.390	2.760	2.340	1.830	1.730	2.060	3.470	2.290	1.300	1.880	2.340	2.800	3.490	2.380
	Volume	12,050	7,440	8,760	8,156	5,407	7,347	12,186	9,656	7,078	9,399	10,357	11,196	11,020	7,000
	Unit Price	0.364	0.371	0.267	0.224	0.206	0.280	0.285	0.237	0.184	0.200	0.226	0.250	0.320	0.340
Petroleum Products	Price	0.003	4.660	4.980	3.600	3.530	4.220	6.270	7.310	6.610	5.570	3.820	10.030	8.980	6.140
	Volume	17	32,950	32,870	41,126	73,943	61,286	89,126	106,596	101,899	134,332	83,118	185,135	121,820	153,600
	Unit Price	0.150	0.141	0.152	0.088	0.048	0.069	0.070	0.069	0.065	0.041	0.046	0.050	0.070	0.040
Chromite	Price	4.060	4.740	5.560	3.290	5.880	15.180	9.050	6.710	5.480	5.600	3.850	8.160	6.760	5.690
	Volume	92,420	103,180	130,240	83,842	148,500	152,591	127,558	129,342	108,450	143,800	89,954	128,543	110,120	113,750
	Unit Price	0.044	0.046	0.043	0.039	0.040	0.099	0.071	0.052	0.051	0.039	0.043	0.060	0.060	0.050
Graphite	Price	6.040	7.190	7.150	6.130	7.070	7.500	11.170	6.980	5.260	4.820	5.560	6.320	5.390	4.940
	Volume	14,720	16,130	13,710	11,141	13,839	15,050	18,503	13,554	10,671	11,182	15,577	16,544	14,310	13,000
	Unit Price	0.410	0.446	0.522	0.550	0.511	0.498	0.604	0.515	0.493	0.431	0.357	0.380	0.380	0.380
Cloves Oil	Price	5.900	3.630	2.750	3.590	1.920	1.750	1.250	1.670	1.640	2.000	2.210	3.660	2.910	4.100
	Volume	1,780	1,140	1,030	1,329	1,070	827	613	1,460	994	1,388	1,294	1,577	1,020	1,500
	Unit Price	3.315	3.184	2.670	2.701	1.794	2.116	2.039	1.144	1.650	1.441	1.708	2.320	2.850	2.730

Source: Central Bank and Ministry of Finance.

*Estimates

**Provisional

69

Table 10: Monthly Exchange Rate

	FF Moyenne de la période	FF Fin de période	USD Moyenne de la période	USD Fin de période	GBP Moyenne de la période	GBP Fin de période	DEM Moyenne de la période	DEM Fin de période	JPY Moyenne de la période	JPY Fin de période	DTS Moyenne de la période	DTS Fin de période
Moyenne 1994	559.3	561.4	3067.2	3057.6	4723.3	4726.9	1914.5	1921.6	30.3	30.5	4414.1	4423.3
Janvier 1995	753.7	809.0	3993.5	4250.0	6284.0	6753.5	2605.3	2808.5	40.0	43.0	5852.3	6265.3
Février	804.7	816.0	4206.5	4197.9	6615.1	6639.8	2795.7	2883.2	42.8	43.4	6219.0	6279.4
Mars	826.3	846.0	4134.9	4160.2	6607.1	6669.0	2927.8	2946.4	45.3	46.3	6330.8	6476.0
Avril	828.8	846.0	4021.3	4113.3	6469.3	6628.4	2908.0	2984.5	47.8	49.2	6335.1	6495.1
Mai	854.5	866.0	4250.3	4236.9	6755.3	6772.6	3027.0	3053.7	50.1	51.0	6646.1	6671.3
Juin	883.0	903.0	4345.8	4411.2	6934.6	6990.6	3103.1	3166.6	51.5	51.8	6797.8	6886.5
Juillet	917.4	932.0	4442.0	4468.0	7082.8	7137.7	3194.0	3224.8	51.0	50.5	6918.5	6947.0
Août	944.8	948.0	4682.0	4797.8	7351.4	7433.3	3251.5	3269.0	49.8	49.3	7085.6	7140.1
Septembre	941.5	919.0	4750.7	4506.3	7395.1	7114.0	3247.9	3172.4	47.5	45.2	7052.1	6772.7
Octobre	841.9	934.0	4163.6	4588.3	6569.2	7239.0	2942.1	3284.4	41.4	45.2	6236.7	6827.2
Novembre	868.1	836.0	4239.5	4120.2	6637.7	6387.5	2995.0	2871.2	41.6	40.8	6336.3	6123.0
Décembre	797.2	697.0	3957.5	3423.0	6087.5	5312.5	2746.1	2302.9	38.9	33.3	5882.7	5085.5
Moyenne 1995	855.2	862.7	4265.6	4272.8	6732.4	6756.5	2978.7	2997.3	45.6	45.7	6474.4	6497.4
Janvier 1996	792.3	788.0	3959.9	4025.9	6066.0	6055.0	2713.4	2708.4	37.6	37.6	5814.6	5854.3
Février	796.7	762.0	4018.1	3800.1	6167.6	5852.9	2740.5	2618.6	38.0	36.6	5891.3	5611.6
Mars	777.5	784.0	3932.3	3954.5	6008.8	6030.5	2663.0	2676.5	37.2	37.2	5754.1	5854.3
Avril	771.0	758.0	3933.2	3919.2	5966.0	5910.1	2617.9	2557.0	36.6	36.9	5680.5	5308.0
Mai	768.3	785.0	3986.4	4100.8	6024.3	6202.7	2599.5	2656.8	37.6	38.1	5757.3	5874.9
Juin	789.9	792.0	4090.6	4080.8	6300.8	6318.2	2677.6	2679.1	37.6	37.2	5901.3	5890.0
Juillet	791.4	790.0	4036.6	3962.6	6270.3	6171.1	2679.9	2682.0	36.9	36.7	5852.8	5795.4
Août	786.2	793.0	3974.9	4023.7	6161.2	6261.9	2682.8	2713.6	36.9	37.0	5796.6	5852.9
Septembre	798.1	803.0	4089.0	4141.1	6374.9	6465.0	2719.0	2714.6	37.3	37.3	5924.9	5973.0
Octobre	798.0	798.0	4128.0	4074.1	6524.2	6546.0	2698.7	2698.1	36.8	35.9	5936.9	5886.3
Novembre	818.5	811.0	4182.9	4229.4	6951.9	7113.7	2769.4	2756.2	37.3	37.2	6076.5	6066.7
Décembre	822.4	824.0	4309.6	4328.5	7160.1	7283.3	2779.6	2779.1	37.9	37.5	6199.4	6214.1
Moyenne 1996	792.5	790.7	4053.5	4053.4	6331.3	6350.9	2695.1	2686.7	37.3	37.1	5882.2	5848.5
Janvier 1997	835.2	861.0	4509.6	4764.4	7505.8	7723.2	2818.5	2906.1	38.4	39.1	6386.4	6642.9
Février	862.2	863.0	4867.2	4942.0	7907.4	8000.9	2911.0	2910.4	39.6	40.6	6735.7	6765.2
Mars	865.5	859.0	4956.0	4847.8	7958.4	7905.4	2920.0	2893.1	40.5	39.2	6823.9	6751.0
Avril	860.1	861.0	4945.6	5024.8	8059.2	8157.5	2896.3	2902.0	39.5	39.7	6787.4	6852.3
Mai	837.6	880.0	5012.8	5061.2	8184.6	8289.6	2945.4	2973.9	42.4	43.5	6952.0	7044.2
Juin	879.3	876.0	5121.4	5118.4	8401.5	8532.7	2968.3	2955.7	44.8	44.8	7120.2	7118.2
Juillet	875.4	875.0	5276.2	5437.3	8829.8	8838.4	2953.2	2949.5	45.9	45.7	7267.1	7363.6
Août	879.0	885.0	5466.7	5352.9	8771.6	8679.6	2962.8	2978.8	46.4	44.8	7390.1	7298.5
Septembre	887.6	890.0	5342.9	5266.6	8550.1	8508.9	2983.8	2989.0	44.3	43.5	7257.7	7195.9
Octobre	888.5	889.0	5248.2	5182.4	8538.7	8650.4	2981.3	2977.1	43.4	43.1	7193.3	7238.4
Novembre	892.4	890.0	5165.8	5251.1	8715.9	8811.5	2988.2	2978.6	41.5	41.1	7096.0	7126.8
Décembre	892.4	888.0	5302.9	5284.7	8813.8	8856.0	2987.6	2971.4	41.0	40.6	7183.2	7161.5
Moyenne 1997	871.3	876.4	5101.3	5127.8	8353.1	8412.8	2943.0	2948.8	42.3	42.1	7016.1	7046.5

Source: Central Bank and Ministry of Finance.

Table 11: Central Government Operations

(As a percent of GDP)	1984	1985	1986	1987	1988	1989	1990	1991	1992	1993	1994	1995	1996	1997
Total Current Revenues (incl. current grants)	14.4%	13.3%	12.7%	15.3%	13.8%	12.7%	13.3%	9.3%	10.9%	10.7%	8.7%	8.8%	9.4%	11.4%
Total Current Revenues (excl. current grants)	13.6%	12.9%	12.0%	14.7%	13.1%	11.3%	11.8%	8.5%	9.8%	9.7%	8.3%	8.5%	8.6%	9.4%
Direct Taxes	2.2%	1.8%	1.8%	1.6%	1.5%	1.2%	1.5%	1.3%	1.3%	1.6%	1.7%	1.2%	1.6%	1.8%
Indirect Taxes	7.3%	8.3%	7.5%	9.3%	9.0%	7.7%	7.9%	5.5%	7.4%	6.6%	6.0%	7.1%	6.9%	7.3%
On Domestic Goods & Services	3.4%	3.1%	3.3%	3.7%	3.2%	2.6%	2.4%	1.7%	2.9%	2.4%	2.4%	2.4%	2.3%	2.4%
On International Trade	3.9%	5.2%	4.2%	5.7%	5.8%	5.0%	5.5%	3.8%	4.5%	4.2%	3.7%	4.7%	4.6%	5.0%
Nontax Receipts	1.2%	0.6%	0.9%	1.0%	1.0%	1.9%	2.1%	1.1%	1.5%	1.4%	0.9%	0.4%	0.9%	2.3%
Grants,Total Current	0.7%	0.4%	0.7%	0.7%	0.7%	1.4%	1.5%	0.8%	1.1%	0.9%	0.4%	0.2%	0.7%	2.0%
Unclassified tax revenue	3.7%	2.6%	2.5%	3.4%	2.3%	2.0%	1.7%	1.3%	0.8%	1.1%	0.1%	0.0%	0.0%	0.0%
Total current expenditures	11.2%	11.2%	10.8%	11.7%	10.2%	10.0%	9.1%	9.8%	11.8%	12.1%	12.8%	11.3%	10.5%	9.6%
Interest on external debt	1.3%	1.2%	1.2%	1.7%	1.8%	1.1%	1.0%	1.1%	1.4%	3.2%	5.1%	4.6%	3.9%	2.0%
Interest on domestic debt	0.2%	0.3%	0.4%	0.4%	0.3%	0.5%	0.5%	0.9%	2.0%	0.9%	0.3%	0.5%	0.8%	0.3%
Other current transfers	1.6%	1.4%	1.7%	1.7%	1.5%	1.8%	1.6%	1.7%	1.2%	2.0%	1.5%	1.3%	1.4%	1.7%
Consumption	8.1%	8.3%	7.5%	7.9%	6.7%	6.6%	5.9%	6.0%	7.1%	6.1%	5.9%	4.9%	4.4%	5.6%
Wages and Salaries	5.4%	5.4%	4.9%	4.8%	4.5%	4.2%	3.9%	4.4%	4.0%	3.7%	3.4%	3.2%	3.1%	3.3%
Total capital revenues	0.0%	0.0%	0.0%	0.0%	0.0%	0.2%	0.1%	0.2%	0.2%	0.2%	0.1%	0.0%	0.0%	0.0%
Total Capital Expenditures and Net Lending	5.4%	5.1%	4.7%	6.2%	6.1%	8.9%	7.3%	6.0%	7.5%	7.9%	6.6%	6.1%	7.0%	7.1%
Capital Transfers	2.0%	1.6%	1.6%	1.9%	2.0%	4.7%	4.1%	2.8%	4.1%	3.7%	3.2%	3.0%	4.0%	3.8%
Budgetary Investment	3.3%	3.4%	3.1%	4.3%	4.1%	4.1%	3.2%	3.1%	3.5%	4.2%	3.4%	3.1%	3.1%	3.3%
Unclassified expenditures	1.1%	0.9%	0.8%	0.8%	0.8%	0.8%	0.7%	0.7%	0.7%	0.6%	0.4%	0.2%	0.2%	0.3%
Overall Surplus/Deficit, incl. cur. grants	-3.3%	-3.9%	-3.5%	-3.4%	-3.3%	-6.8%	-3.6%	-6.9%	-9.0%	-9.8%	-11.0%	-8.9%	-8.4%	-5.6%
Overall Surplus/Deficit, incl. all grants	-3.3%	-3.9%	-3.5%	-3.4%	-3.3%	-4.1%	-0.7%	-5.5%	-6.6%	-7.2%	-8.4%	-6.2%	-4.9%	-2.4%
Overall Surplus/Deficit, excl. cur. grants	-4.0%	-4.3%	-4.2%	-4.0%	-4.1%	-8.2%	-5.1%	-7.7%	-10.1%	-10.7%	-11.4%	-9.1%	-9.1%	-7.7%
Total Deficit Financing	3.3%	3.9%	3.5%	3.4%	3.3%	6.8%	3.6%	6.9%	9.0%	9.8%	11.0%	8.9%	8.4%	5.6%
External Capital Grants	0.0%	0.0%	0.0%	0.0%	0.0%	2.7%	2.9%	1.3%	2.4%	2.6%	2.6%	2.7%	3.5%	3.2%
External Borrowing (net)	2.2%	2.5%	2.3%	3.6%	3.9%	4.6%	2.1%	3.9%	2.7%	2.9%	1.7%	1.9%	5.0%	2.7%
Domestic Borrowing	1.1%	1.4%	1.2%	-0.3%	-0.6%	-0.5%	-1.4%	1.7%	3.9%	4.3%	6.7%	4.3%	-0.1%	-0.3%
Memorandum:														
As a percent of total revenues:														
Direct Taxes	16.1%	13.6%	14.7%	11.1%	11.4%	10.1%	12.7%	15.0%	12.9%	16.2%	19.8%	14.6%	18.3%	18.7%
Indirect Taxes	53.3%	64.2%	62.6%	63.6%	68.8%	66.8%	66.2%	63.3%	73.9%	66.2%	72.4%	82.9%	79.3%	78.0%
On domestic goods & services	25.0%	24.1%	27.4%	24.9%	24.2%	23.0%	20.0%	19.9%	29.3%	24.0%	28.4%	27.8%	26.0%	25.1%
On international trade	28.3%	40.1%	35.3%	38.7%	44.7%	43.8%	46.2%	43.4%	44.7%	42.2%	44.0%	55.1%	53.3%	52.9%
Nontax Receipts	3.4%	2.0%	2.1%	1.9%	1.9%	4.3%	5.7%	4.1%	3.5%	4.6%	6.1%	2.4%	2.2%	2.8%
Unclassified Tax Revenue	27.2%	20.3%	20.5%	23.3%	17.8%	17.0%	14.3%	14.9%	7.7%	11.4%	1.1%	0.0%	0.0%	0.0%
As a percent of total expenditure:														
Interest on External Debt	7.3%	6.8%	7.4%	9.1%	10.4%	5.7%	6.1%	6.9%	6.9%	15.3%	25.6%	26.3%	21.8%	11.7%
Interest on Domestic Debt	1.2%	1.7%	2.2%	1.9%	1.9%	2.6%	2.8%	5.4%	10.2%	4.1%	1.6%	2.7%	4.5%	1.8%
Other Current Transfers	9.0%	8.4%	10.3%	9.3%	8.6%	8.9%	9.7%	10.4%	6.0%	9.9%	7.6%	7.1%	7.8%	9.7%
Consumption	46.0%	48.5%	46.6%	42.4%	38.9%	33.5%	34.9%	36.9%	35.6%	29.5%	29.9%	28.1%	24.9%	33.1%
o.w. wages and walaries	30.8%	31.2%	30.5%	25.6%	26.4%	21.3%	23.1%	26.5%	19.7%	18.0%	17.0%	18.1%	17.7%	19.2%
Capital expenditure	30.4%	29.4%	28.8%	33.1%	35.7%	45.1%	42.7%	36.4%	37.6%	38.2%	33.3%	34.8%	39.7%	41.7%
Unclassified expenditure	6.1%	5.3%	4.6%	4.2%	4.7%	4.2%	3.9%	4.0%	3.7%	3.0%	1.9%	1.0%	1.2%	2.0%

Source: Ministry of Finance and World Bank staff estimates.

Table 12: Intra and inter Sectoral Allocations of Public Expenditures

En Milliards de FMG	1995 (1 SDR = 6,474.4 FMG)			1996 (1 SDR = 5,887.2 FMG)			1997** (1 SDR = 7,111.0 FMG)			1998** (1 SDR = 7,393.2 FMG)		
	Fonction.*	Invest.	Total	Fonction.*	Invest.	Total	Fonction.*	Invest.	Total	Fonction.*	Invest.	Total
Total Dépenses	1,523.40	850.40	2,373.80	1,703.80	1,179.60	2,883.40	1,679.50	1,399.10	3,078.60	2,400.29	1,818.90	4,219.19
Total Recettes	1,179.40	362.30	1,541.70	1,520.70	569.80	2,090.50	1,763.70	628.80	2,392.50	2,251.00	716.60	2,967.60
Education	188.20	84.00	272.20	187.70	85.40	273.10	292.17	72.91	365.08	299.90	172.81	472.70
. Primaire	120.36	32.29	152.65	135.64	38.38	174.03	157.02	46.22	203.23	167.74	115.62	283.36
. Secondaire	27.74	27.10	54.84	8.96	38.89	47.85	81.43	14.69	96.13	80.42	9.68	90.10
. Supérieure	40.10	24.61	64.71	43.10	8.13	51.23	53.72	12.00	65.72	51.73	47.51	99.24
Santé	84.40	120.00	204.40	80.20	125.70	205.90	140.25	217.17	357.42	129.42	313.21	442.63
. Santé de base	73.50	56.00	129.50	65.60	109.00	174.60	50.31	113.05	163.37	54.35	150.16	204.52
. Autres	10.90	64.00	74.90	14.60	16.70	31.30	89.94	104.11	194.05	75.07	163.05	238.11
Infrastructures	10.90	281.40	292.30	8.20	284.24	292.44	71.74	401.65	473.39	21.46	602.49	623.95
Agriculture & Ress. Naturelles	12.50	149.00	161.50	49.20	281.40	330.60	65.27	317.09	382.36	55.03	569.25	624.29
Défense	115.90	2.61	118.51	200.80	0.17	200.97	188.18	12.94	201.12	183.40	13.99	197.39
Autres	423.60	213.39	636.99	418.50	402.69	821.19	553.38	377.34	930.73	1,310.38	147.15	1,457.53
Intérêts de la dette	687.90	0.00	687.90	759.20	0.00	759.20	368.50	0.00	368.50	400.70	0.00	400.70
Total	1,523.40	850.40	2,373.80	1,703.80	1,179.60	2,883.40	1,679.50	1,399.10	3,078.60	2,400.29	1,818.90	4,219.19

(Pourcentage par rapport au Total des Dépenses)

	Fonction.*	Invest.	Total	Fonction.*	Invest.	Total	Fonction.*	Invest.	Total	Fonction.*	Invest.	Total
Total Dépenses	64.18%	35.82%	100.00%	59.09%	40.91%	100.00%	54.55%	45.45%	100.00%	56.89%	43.11%	100.00%
Total Recettes	49.7%	15.3%	64.9%	52.7%	19.8%	72.5%	57.3%	20.4%	77.7%	53.4%	17.0%	70.3%
Education	7.93%	3.54%	11.47%	6.51%	2.96%	9.47%	9.49%	2.37%	11.86%	7.11%	4.10%	11.20%
. Primaire	5.07%	1.36%	6.43%	4.70%	1.33%	6.04%	5.10%	1.50%	6.60%	3.98%	2.74%	6.72%
. Secondaire	1.17%	1.14%	2.31%	0.31%	1.35%	1.66%	2.65%	0.48%	3.12%	1.91%	0.23%	2.14%
. Supérieure	1.69%	1.04%	2.73%	1.49%	0.28%	1.78%	1.74%	0.39%	2.13%	1.23%	1.13%	2.35%
Santé	3.56%	5.06%	8.61%	2.78%	4.36%	7.14%	4.56%	7.05%	11.61%	3.07%	7.42%	10.49%
. Santé de base	3.10%	2.36%	5.46%	2.28%	3.78%	6.06%	1.63%	3.67%	5.31%	1.29%	3.56%	4.85%
. Autres	0.46%	2.70%	3.16%	0.51%	0.58%	1.09%	2.92%	3.38%	6.30%	1.78%	3.86%	5.64%
Infrastructures	0.46%	11.85%	12.31%	0.28%	9.86%	10.14%	2.33%	13.05%	15.38%	0.51%	14.28%	14.79%
Agriculture & Ress. Naturelles	0.53%	6.28%	6.80%	1.71%	9.76%	11.47%	2.12%	10.30%	12.42%	1.30%	13.49%	14.80%
Défense	4.88%	0.11%	4.99%	6.96%	0.01%	6.97%	6.11%	0.42%	6.53%	4.35%	0.33%	4.68%
Autres	17.84%	8.99%	26.83%	14.51%	13.97%	28.48%	17.98%	12.26%	30.23%	31.06%	3.49%	34.55%
Intérêts de la dette	28.98%	0.00%	28.98%	26.33%	0.00%	26.33%	11.97%	0.00%	11.97%	9.50%	0.00%	9.50%
Total	64.18%	35.82%	100.00%	59.09%	40.91%	100.00%	54.55%	45.45%	100.00%	56.89%	43.11%	100.00%

Emploi public et dépenses de personnel

	1995		1996		1997		1998	
Solde	444.50 Mds FMG		523.10 Mds FMG		624.50 Mds FMG		734.00 Mds FMG	
Emploi Public (Nombre)	121,266		120,530		135,488		135,488	
Pourcentage / Population	13,126,000	0.92%	13,494,000	0.89%	13,872,000	0.97%	14,260,000	0.95%
Percentage / Active Population	6,956,780	1.74%	7,151,820	1.69%	7,352,160	1.84%	7,557,800	1.79%

* Fonctionnement = Solde + Biens et Services + Transferts   ** Prévisions de décaissements   Mds = Milliards = Billions

Source: Ministry of Budget and World Bank staff estimates.

Table 13: Summary Annual Accounts of the Financial System, 1986-2015

(In billions of Malagasy francs; end of period) -- STOCKS

	1986	1987	1988	1989	1990	1991	1992	1993	1994	1995	1996	1997
Net foreign assets	-27.95	137.57	297.17	381.87	178.48	27.09	274.34	349.71	702.57	864.89	1491.13	2075.50
Central Bank, net	-49.64	83.90	232.85	288.53	111.90	-103.13	112.11	136.19	223.57	359.69	1029.24	1543.48
Commercial banks, net	21.70	53.67	64.32	93.34	66.59	130.22	162.23	213.51	479.00	505.21	461.89	532.02
Net domestic assets	1272.76	2006.28	2319.53	2601.22	2842.06	3658.98	1242.40	1457.30	2135.52	2263.72	2220.82	2218.16
Total domestic credit	826.13	891.19	888.87	919.87	1029.87	1183.41	1621.29	1904.97	2193.55	2374.96	2383.90	2517.62
Credit to Government, net	376.99	365.00	342.65	312.54	251.47	308.85	683.29	825.29	837.06	811.27	784.52	725.52
Of which: Central Bank	394.28	400.84	375.50	309.65	292.47	392.99	787.67	742.53	710.48	725.84	687.38	483.99
Credit to the economy	449.14	526.19	546.22	607.33	778.39	874.56	938.00	1079.67	1356.49	1563.69	1599.38	1792.10
Public enterprises	215.01	228.37	215.14	199.82	165.95	142.73	111.07	90.43	11.58	12.62	14.13	11.58
Private sector	234.13	297.82	331.09	407.51	612.45	731.82	826.93	989.24	1344.91	1551.07	1585.26	1780.52
Other items, net	446.64	1115.09	1430.65	1681.35	1812.20	2475.57	-378.88	-447.67	-58.03	-111.25	-163.08	-299.46
Accumulated BCRM gains (-)/losses	194.35	306.65	393.52	561.52	588.81	684.62	0.00	1.62	-13.59	-2.62	16.93	17.20
Exchange valuation gains (-)/losses	405.58	1058.68	1286.35	1413.11	1489.60	2087.20	0.00	10.34	311.10	345.83	355.56	250.60
Other items (assets +)	-153.30	-250.23	-249.22	-293.28	-266.22	-296.24	-378.88	-459.63	-355.54	-454.45	-535.57	-567.26
Broad Money	448.30	527.37	633.93	822.74	825.27	1034.76	1240.29	1564.87	2339.37	2717.32	3209.75	4018.51
Money supply	304.06	386.61	469.58	613.08	588.58	767.98	915.03	1038.00	1601.03	1842.30	2180.71	2500.27
Currency	113.24	140.28	171.17	216.64	214.93	287.29	317.23	378.74	614.53	758.70	831.24	875.10
Demand deposits	190.82	246.33	298.41	396.44	373.65	480.68	597.80	659.26	986.49	1083.60	1349.46	1625.18
Quasi money	144.24	140.76	164.34	209.66	236.69	266.78	325.26	526.87	738.34	875.02	1029.04	1518.23
Of which: foreign currency deposits								19.21	230.70	284.63	285.15	328.21
Long-term foreign liabilities	796.52	1616.48	1982.77	2160.35	2195.27	2651.31	276.46	242.14	498.73	411.29	502.20	698.85
Central Bank	790.78	1609.17	1977.86	2156.97	2194.22	2650.25	270.59	235.86	477.53	385.27	477.29	670.15
Commercial banks	5.74	7.31	4.91	3.38	1.05	1.06	5.86	6.28	21.20	26.02	24.91	28.69

Source: Central Bank and IMF.

73

Table 14: Interest Rates 1991-1996

	1991	1992	1993	1994	1995	1996
Taux directeur de la Banque centrale (fin de période)	12.00	12.00	12.00	23.75	33.00	17.00
Taux de la Banque Centrale pour avance statutaire au Trésor (fin de période)	13.00	13.00	12.73	12.73	33.00	17.00
Taux de la Banque centrale pour les dépôts du Trésor (fin de période)	12.00	12.00	3.50	3.50	2.11	2.11
Taux débiteurs de base minimum des Banques de dépôts (fin de periode)	15.00	15.00	13.00	17.00	19.63	19.00
Taux débiteurs de base maximum des Banques de dépôts (fin de période)	15.50	16.17	15.50	21.00	28.58	20.46
Taux débiteurs minimum des Banques de dépôts pour les créances sur export (fin de période)		11.04	11.75	11.50	10.36	10.00
Taux débiteurs maximum des Banques de dépôts pour les créances sur export (fin de période)		14.15	14.50	20.02	31.25	23.96
Taux débiteurs mimimun des Banques de dépôts pour financement de marchandises (fin de période)		16.42	15.40	21.73	26.27	21.90
Taux débiteurs maximum des Banques de dépôts pour financement de marchandises (fin de période)		21.14	20.19	25.94	32.58	27.69
Taux débiteurs minimum des Banques de dépôts pour découvert et avance (fin de période)		19.34	20.40	18.28	21.77	21.67
Taux débiteurs maximum des Banques de dépôts pour découvert et avance (fin de période)		21.78	21.05	28.03	33.95	28.60
Taux débiteurs minimum des Banques de dépôts pour crédit de campagne (fin de période)		15.06	14.99	18.30	18.23	18.40
Taux débiteurs maximum des Banques de dépôts pour crédit de campagne (fin de période)		21.19	20.75	23.32	33.89	29.46
Taux créditeurs minimum des Banques de dépôts pour les dépôts à vue (fin de période)		2.26	1.50	1.58	1.90	1.45
Taux créditeurs maximum des Banques de dépôts pour les dépôts à vue (fin de période)		2.80	30.60	2.72	7.00	7.00
Taux créditeurs minimum des Banques de dépôts pour les dépôts à plus de 2 ans (fin de période)		13.80	12.40	13.65	10.46	10.00
Taux créditeurs maximum des Banques de dépôts pour les dépôts à plus de 2 ans (fin de période)		15.32	15.34	17.75	18.00	18.00
Taux créditeurs minimum des Banques de dépôts pour les dépôts en dévises à terme (fin de période)				2.08	2.50	2.17
Taux créditeurs maximum des Banques de dépôts pour les dépôts en dévises à terme (fin de période)				5.32	6.45	3.50

Source: Central Bank.

Table 15: Petroleum Products: Retail Prices, Imports, and Consumption, 1990-1996

	1990	1991	1992	1993	1994	1995	1996
RETAIL PRICES							
Gaz (12.5 kg)	13,654	13,654	13,654	11,525	25,000	25,000	34,000
Premium Gasoline (FMG/liter)	949	959	974	954	2,110	1,930	2,180
Gasoline (FMG/liter)	822	832	848	822	1,240	1,610	1,860
Kerosene (FMG/liter)	349	366	410	476	513	1,190	1,340
Diesel (FMG/liter)	422	483	518	592	727	1,320	1,500
IMPORTS							
Gaz (Metric Tons)	0	0	0	0	945	0	0
Gasoline (M3)	15,023	0	0	3,991	34,468	12,430	24,388
Kérosène (M3)	23,876	10,968	**4,843**	1,004	24,158	1,500	18,562
Diesel (M3)	110,912	94,094	**94,659**	122,743	153,289	116,959	138,657
Petroleum Oil (M3)	345,251	391,044	**400,737**	475,485	331,316	520,911	464,976
CONSUMPTION							
Gaz (Metric Tons)	2,943	2,876	2,749	3,214	3,811	3,559	3,838
Premium Gasoline (M3)	4,021	3,494	4,296	6,572	3,709	3,623	5,569
Gasoline (M3)	75,788	68,301	74,002	82,658	87,338	95,893	103,988
Fuel Oil (M3)	138,806	128,426	133,127	180,208	121,305	222,983	149,664
Jet (M3)	22,109	19,268	17,221	29,665	23,361	28,967	22,859
PL (M3)	43,123	42,864	43,510	45,302	45,340	45,525	43,535
Diesel (M3)	193,188	195,963	217,077	217,366	250,551	260,822	265,733

Source: Ministry of Finance.

Distributors of World Bank Group Publications

Prices and credit terms vary from country to country. Consult your local distributor before placing an order.

ARGENTINA
World Publications SA
Av. Cordoba 1877
1120 Ciudad de Buenos Aires
Tel: (54 11) 4815-8156
Fax: (54 11) 4815-8156
E-mail: wpbooks@infovia.com.ar

AUSTRALIA, FIJI, PAPUA NEW GUINEA, SOLOMON ISLANDS, VANUATU, AND SAMOA
D.A. Information Services
648 Whitehorse Road
Mitcham 3132, Victoria
Tel: (61) 3 9210 7777
Fax: (61) 3 9210 7788
E-mail: service@dadirect.com.au
URL: http://www.dadirect.com.au

AUSTRIA
Gerold and Co.
Weihburggasse 26
A-1011 Wien
Tel: (43 1) 512-47-31-0
Fax: (43 1) 512-47-31-29
URL: http://www.gerold.co/at.online

BANGLADESH
Micro Industries Development
Assistance Society (MIDAS)
House 5, Road 16
Dhanmondi R/Area
Dhaka 1209
Tel: (880 2) 326427
Fax: (880 2) 811188

BELGIUM
Jean De Lannoy
Av. du Roi 202
1060 Brussels
Tel: (32 2) 538-5169
Fax: (32 2) 538-0841

BRAZIL
Publicacões Tecnicas Internacionais
Ltda.
Rua Peixoto Gomide, 209
01409 Sao Paulo, SP.
Tel: (55 11) 259-6644
Fax: (55 11) 258-6990
E-mail: postmaster@pti.uol.br
URL: http://www.uol.br

CANADA
Renouf Publishing Co. Ltd.
5369 Canotek Road
Ottawa, Ontario K1J 9J3
Tel: (613) 745-2665
Fax: (613) 745-7660
E-mail:
order.dept@renoufbooks.com
URL: http:// www.renoufbooks.com

CHINA
China Financial & Economic
Publishing House
8, Da Fo Si Dong Jie
Beijing
Tel: (86 10) 6401-7365
Fax: (86 10) 6401-7365

China Book Import Centre
P.O. Box 2825
Beijing

Chinese Corporation for Promotion
of Humanities
52, You Fang Hu Tong,
Xuan Nei Da Jie
Beijing
Tel: (86 10) 660 72 494
Fax: (86 10) 660 72 494

COLOMBIA
Infoenlace Ltda.
Carrera 6 No. 51-21
Apartado Aereo 34270
Santafé de Bogotá, D.C.
Tel: (57 1) 285-2798
Fax: (57 1) 285-2798

COTE D'IVOIRE
Center d'Edition et de Diffusion
Africaines (CEDA)
04 B.P. 541
Abidjan 04
Tel: (225) 24 6510; 24 6511
Fax: (225) 25 0567

CYPRUS
Center for Applied Research
Cyprus College
6, Diogenes Street, Engomi
P.O. Box 2006
Nicosia
Tel: (357 2) 59-0730
Fax: (357 2) 66-2051

CZECH REPUBLIC
USIS, NIS Prodejna
Havelkova 22
130 00 Prague 3
Tel: (420 2) 2423 1486
Fax: (420 2) 2423 1114
URL: http://www.nis.cz/

DENMARK
SamfundsLitteratur
Rosenoerns Allé 11
DK-1970 Frederiksberg C
Tel: (45 35) 351942
Fax: (45 35) 357822
URL: http://www.sl.cbs.dk

ECUADOR
Libri Mundi
Libreria Internacional
P.O. Box 17-01-3029
Juan Leon Mera 851
Quito
Tel: (593 2) 521-606; (593 2) 544-185
Fax: (593 2) 504-209
E-mail: librimu1@librimundi.com.ec
E-mail: librimu2@librimundi.com.ec

CODEU
Ruiz de Castilla 763, Edif. Expocolor
Primer piso, Of. #2
Quito
Tel/Fax: (593 2) 507-383; 253-091
E-mail: codeu@impsat.net.ec

EGYPT, ARAB REPUBLIC OF
Al Ahram Distribution Agency
Al Galaa Street
Cairo
Tel: (20 2) 578-6083
Fax: (20 2) 578-6833

The Middle East Observer
41, Sherif Street
Cairo
Tel: (20 2) 393-9732
Fax: (20 2) 393-9732

FINLAND
Akateeminen Kirjakauppa
P.O. Box 128
FIN-00101 Helsinki
Tel: (358 0) 121 4418
Fax: (358 0) 121-4435
E-mail: akatilaus@stockmann.fi
URL: http://www.akateeminen.com

FRANCE
Editions Eska; DBJ
48, rue Gay Lussac
75005 Paris
Tel: (33-1) 55-42-73-08
Fax: (33-1) 43-29-91-67

GERMANY
UNO-Verlag
Poppelsdorfer Allee 55
53116 Bonn
Tel: (49 228) 949020
Fax: (49 228) 217492
URL: http://www.uno-verlag.de
E-mail: unoverlag@aol.com

GHANA
Epp Books Services
P.O. Box 44
TUC
Accra
Tel: 223 21 778843
Fax: 223 21 779099

GREECE
Papasotiriou S.A.
35, Stournara Str.
106 82 Athens
Tel: (30 1) 364-1826
Fax: (30 1) 364-8254

HAITI
Culture Diffusion
5, Rue Capois
C.P. 257
Port-au-Prince
Tel: (509) 23 9260
Fax: (509) 23 4858

HONG KONG, CHINA; MACAO
Asia 2000 Ltd.
Sales & Circulation Department
302 Seabird House
22-28 Wyndham Street, Central
Hong Kong, China
Tel: (852) 2530-1409
Fax: (852) 2526-1107
E-mail: sales@asia2000.com.hk
URL: http://www.asia2000.com.hk

HUNGARY
Euro Info Service
Margitszgeti Europa Haz
H-1138 Budapest
Tel: (36 1) 350 80 24, 350 80 25
Fax: (36 1) 350 90 32
E-mail: euroinfo@mail.matav.hu

INDIA
Allied Publishers Ltd.
751 Mount Road
Madras - 600 002
Tel: (91 44) 852-3938
Fax: (91 44) 852-0649

INDONESIA
Pt. Indira Limited
Jalan Borobudur 20
P.O. Box 181
Jakarta 10320
Tel: (62 21) 390-4290
Fax: (62 21) 390-4289

IRAN
Ketab Sara Co. Publishers
Khaled Eslamboli Ave., 6th Street
Delafrooz Alley No. 8
P.O. Box 15745-733
Tehran 15117
Tel: (98 21) 8717819; 8716104
Fax: (98 21) 8712479
E-mail: ketab-sara@neda.net.ir

Kowkab Publishers
P.O. Box 19575-511
Tehran
Tel: (98 21) 258-3723
Fax: (98 21) 258-3723

IRELAND
Government Supplies Agency
Oifig an tSoláthair
4-5 Harcourt Road
Dublin 2
Tel: (353 1) 661-3111
Fax: (353 1) 475-2670

ISRAEL
Yozmot Literature Ltd.
P.O. Box 56055
3 Yohanan Hasandlar Street
Tel Aviv 61560
Tel: (972 3) 5285-397
Fax: (972 3) 5285-397

R.O.Y. International
PO Box 13056
Tel Aviv 61130
Tel: (972 3) 649 9469
Fax: (972 3) 648 6039
E-mail: royil@netvision.net.il
URL: http://www.royint.co.il

Palestinian Authority/Middle East
Index Information Services
P.O.B. 19502 Jerusalem
Tel: (972 2) 6271219
Fax: (972 2) 6271634

ITALY, LIBERIA
Licosa Commissionaria Sansoni SPA
Via Duca Di Calabria, 1/1
Casella Postale 552
50125 Firenze
Tel: (39 55) 645-415
Fax: (39 55) 641-257
E-mail: licosa@ftbcc.it
URL: http://www.ftbcc.it/licosa

JAMAICA
Ian Randle Publishers Ltd.
206 Old Hope Road, Kingston 6
Tel: 876-927-2085
Fax: 876-977-0243
E-mail: irpl@colis.com

JAPAN
Eastern Book Service
3-13 Hongo 3-chome, Bunkyo-ku
Tokyo 113
Tel: (81 3) 3818-0861
Fax: (81 3) 3818-0864
E-mail: orders@svt-ebs.co.jp
URL:
http://www.bekkoame.or.jp/~svt-ebs

KENYA
Africa Book Service (E.A.) Ltd.
Quaran House, Mfangano Street
P.O. Box 45245
Nairobi
Tel: (254 2) 223 641
Fax: (254 2) 330 272

Legacy Books
Loita House
Mezzanine 1
P.O. Box 68077
Nairobi
Tel: (254) 2-330853, 221426
Fax: (254) 2-330854, 561654
E-mail: Legacy@form-net.com

KOREA, REPUBLIC OF
Dayang Books Trading Co.
International Division
783-20, Pangba Bon-Dong,
Socho-ku
Seoul
Tel: (82 2) 536-9555
Fax: (82 2) 536-0025
E-mail: seamap@chollian.net

Eulyoo Publishing Co., Ltd.
46-1, Susong-Dong
Jongro-Gu
Seoul
Tel: (82 2) 734-3515
Fax: (82 2) 732-9154

LEBANON
Librairie du Liban
P.O. Box 11-9232
Beirut
Tel: (961 9) 217 944
Fax: (961 9) 217 434
E-mail: hsayegh@librairie-du-liban.com.lb
URL: http://www.librairie-du-liban.com.lb

MALAYSIA
University of Malaya Cooperative
Bookshop, Limited
P.O. Box 1127
Jalan Pantai Baru
59700 Kuala Lumpur
Tel: (60 3) 756-5000
Fax: (60 3) 755-4424
E-mail: umkoop@tm.net.my

MEXICO
INFOTEC
Av. San Fernando No. 37
Col. Toriello Guerra
14050 Mexico, D.F.
Tel: (52 5) 624-2800
Fax: (52 5) 624-2822
E-mail: infotec@rtn.net.mx
URL: http://rtn.net.mx

Mundi-Prensa Mexico S.A. de C.V.
c/Rio Panuco, 141-Colonia
Cuauhtemoc
06500 Mexico, D.F.
Tel: (52 5) 533-5658
Fax: (52 5) 514-6799

NEPAL
Everest Media International Services
(P.) Ltd.
GPO Box 5443
Kathmandu
Tel: (977 1) 416 026
Fax: (977 1) 224 431

NETHERLANDS
De Lindeboom/Internationale
Publicaties b.v.-
P.O. Box 202, 7480 AE Haaksbergen
Tel: (31 53) 574-0004
Fax: (31 53) 572-9296
E-mail: lindeboo@worldonline.nl
URL: http://www.worldonline.nl/~lindeboo

NEW ZEALAND
EBSCO NZ Ltd.
Private Mail Bag 99914
New Market
Auckland
Tel: (64 9) 524-8119
Fax: (64 9) 524-8067

Oasis Official
P.O. Box 3627
Wellington
Tel: (64 4) 499 1551
Fax: (64 4) 499 1972
E-mail: oasis@actrix.gen.nz
URL: http://www.oasisbooks.co.nz/

NIGERIA
University Press Limited
Three Crowns Building Jericho
Private Mail Bag 5095
Ibadan
Tel: (234 22) 41-1356
Fax: (234 22) 41-2056

PAKISTAN
Mirza Book Agency
65, Shahrah-e-Quaid-e-Azam
Lahore 54000
Tel: (92 42) 735 3601
Fax: (92 42) 576 3714

Oxford University Press
5 Bangalore Town
Sharae Faisal
PO Box 13033
Karachi-75350
Tel: (92 21) 446307
Fax: (92 21) 4547640
E-mail: ouppak@TheOffice.net

Pak Book Corporation
Aziz Chambers 21, Queen's Road
Lahore
Tel: (92 42) 636 3222; 636 0885
Fax: (92 42) 636 2328
E-mail: pbc@brain.net.pk

PERU
Editorial Desarrollo SA
Apartado 3824, Ica 242 OF. 106
Lima 1
Tel: (51 14) 285380
Fax: (51 14) 286628

PHILIPPINES
International Booksource Center Inc.
1127-A Antipolo St, Barangay,
Venezuela
Makati City
Tel: (63 2) 896 6501; 6505; 6507
Fax: (63 2) 896 1741

POLAND
International Publishing Service
Ul. Piekna 31/37
00-677 Warzawa
Tel: (48 2) 628-6089
Fax: (48 2) 621-7255
E-mail: books%ips@ikp.atm.com.pl
URL:
http://www.ipscg.waw.pl/ips/export

PORTUGAL
Livraria Portugal
Apartado 2681, Rua Do Carm
o 70-74
1200 Lisbon
Tel: (1) 347-4982
Fax: (1) 347-0264

ROMANIA
Compani De Librarii Bucuresti S.A.
Str. Lipscani no. 26, sector 3
Bucharest
Tel: (40 1) 313 9645
Fax: (40 1) 312 4000

RUSSIAN FEDERATION
Isdatelstvo <Ves Mir>
9a, Kolpachniy Pereulok
Moscow 101831
Tel: (7 095) 917 87 49
Fax: (7 095) 917 92 59
ozimarin@glasnet.ru

**SINGAPORE; TAIWAN, CHINA
MYANMAR; BRUNEI**
Hemisphere Publication Services
41 Kallang Pudding Road #04-03
Golden Wheel Building
Singapore 349316
Tel: (65) 741-5166
Fax: (65) 742-9356
E-mail: ashgate@asianconnect.com

SLOVENIA
Gospodarski vestnik Publishing
Group
Dunajska cesta 5
1000 Ljubljana
Tel: (386 61) 133 83 47; 132 12 30
Fax: (386 61) 133 80 30
E-mail: repansekj@gvestnik.si

SOUTH AFRICA, BOTSWANA
For single titles:
Oxford University Press Southern
Africa
Vasco Boulevard, Goodwood
P.O. Box 12119, N1 City 7463
Cape Town
Tel: (27 21) 595 4400
Fax: (27 21) 595 4430
E-mail: oxford@oup.co.za

For subscription orders:
International Subscription Service
P.O. Box 41095
Craighall
Johannesburg 2024
Tel: (27 11) 880-1448
Fax: (27 11) 880-6248
E-mail: iss@is.co.za

SPAIN
Mundi-Prensa Libros, S.A.
Castello 37
28001 Madrid
Tel: (34 91) 4 363700
Fax: (34 91) 5 753998
E-mail: libreria@mundiprensa.es
URL: http://www.mundiprensa.com/

Mundi-Prensa Barcelona
Consell de Cent, 391
08009 Barcelona
Tel: (34 3) 488-3492
Fax: (34 3) 487-7659
E-mail: barcelona@mundiprensa.es

SRI LANKA, THE MALDIVES
Lake House Bookshop
100, Sir Chittampalam Gardiner
Mawatha
Colombo 2
Tel: (94 1) 32105
Fax: (94 1) 432104
E-mail: LHL@sri.lanka.net

SWEDEN
Wennergren-Williams AB
P. O. Box 1305
S-171 25 Solna
Tel: (46 8) 705-97-50
Fax: (46 8) 27-00-71
E-mail: mail@wwi.se

SWITZERLAND
Librairie Payot Service Institutionnel
C(tm)tes-de-Montbenon 30
1002 Lausanne
Tel: (41 21) 341-3229
Fax: (41 21) 341-3235

ADECO Van Diermen
EditionsTechniques
Ch. de Lacuez 41
CH1807 Blonay
Tel: (41 21) 943 2673
Fax: (41 21) 943 3605

THAILAND
Central Books Distribution
306 Silom Road
Bangkok 10500
Tel: (66 2) 2336930-9
Fax: (66 2) 237-8321

**TRINIDAD & TOBAGO
AND THE CARRIBBEAN**
Systematics Studies Ltd.
St. Augustine Shopping Center
Eastern Main Road, St. Augustine
Trinidad & Tobago, West Indies
Tel: (868) 645-8466
Fax: (868) 645-8467
E-mail: tobe@trinidad.net

UGANDA
Gustro Ltd.
PO Box 9997, Madhvani Building
Plot 16/4 Jinja Rd.
Kampala
Tel: (256 41) 251 467
Fax: (256 41) 251 468
E-mail: gus@swiftuganda.com

UNITED KINGDOM
Microinfo Ltd.
P.O. Box 3, Omega Park, Alton,
Hampshire GU34 2PG
England
Tel: (44 1420) 86848
Fax: (44 1420) 89889
E-mail: wbank@microinfo.co.uk
URL: http://www.microinfo.co.uk

The Stationery Office
51 Nine Elms Lane
London SW8 5DR
Tel: (44 171) 873-8400
Fax: (44 171) 873-8242
URL: http://www.the-stationery-office.co.uk/

VENEZUELA
Tecni-Ciencia Libros, S.A.
Centro Cuidad Comercial Tamanco
Nivel C2, Caracas
Tel: (58 2) 959 5547; 5035; 0016
Fax: (58 2) 959 5636

ZAMBIA
University Bookshop, University of
Zambia
Great East Road Campus
P.O. Box 32379
Lusaka
Tel: (260 1) 252 576
Fax: (260 1) 253 952

ZIMBABWE
Academic and Baobab Books (Pvt.)
Ltd.
4 Conald Road, Graniteside
P.O. Box 567
Harare
Tel: 263 4 755035
Fax: 263 4 781913